THE ROOTS OF VIOLENCE

CODEPENDENCE
Coping with Addiction, Sadism and Abuse

EIGHT DYNAMIC PATTERNS OF LIVING
Base Elements of True Civilization

EMOTIONAL FLOW
A Holistic Approach to Healing Sadism

LOVE OR LAWS?
When Law Punishes Life

MINOTAUR UNVEILED
A Historical Assessment of Adult-Child Sexual Interaction

NATURAL ORDER
Thesis, Antithesis and Synthesis in Human Evolution

PEDOPHILIA REVISITED
The Making of a Crime for Justifying Lacking Social Policy

THE COMMERCIAL EXPLOITATION OF ABUSE
A Study on Social Policy

THE LEGAL SPLIT IN CHILD PROTECTION
Overcoming the Double Standard

THE ROOTS OF VIOLENCE
Why Humans Are Not by Nature Violent

THE ROOTS OF VIOLENCE

Why Humans Are Not By Nature Violent

Peter Fritz Walter

Published by Sirius-C Media Galaxy LLC

3511 Silverside Road, Suite 105, Wilmington, DE 19810, USA

Essays on Law, Policy and Psychiatry, Vol. 10

Set in Avenir Light and Trajan Pro

Designed by Peter Fritz Walter

ISBN 978-1-984071-76-7

Publishing Categories
Psychology / Psychopathology / General

Publisher Contact Information
publisher@sirius-c-publishing.com
http://sirius-c-publishing.com

Author Contact Information
pfw@peterfritzwalter.com

About Dr. Peter Fritz Walter
http://peterfritzwalter.com

ABOUT THE AUTHOR

Parallel to an international law career in Germany, Switzerland and the United States, Dr. Peter Fritz Walter (Pierre) focused upon fine art, cookery, astrology, musical performance, social sciences and humanities.

He started writing essays as an adolescent and received a high school award for creative writing and editorial work for the school magazine.

After finalizing his law diplomas, he graduated with an LL.M. in European Integration at Saarland University, Germany, in 1982, and with a Doctor of Law title from University of Geneva, Switzerland, in 1987.

He then took courses in psychology at the University of Geneva and interviewed a number of psychotherapists in Lausanne and Geneva, Switzerland. His interest was intensified through a hypnotherapy with an Ericksonian American hypnotherapist in Lausanne. This led him to the recovery and healing of his inner child.

After a second career as a corporate trainer and personal coach, Pierre retired in 2004 as a full-time writer, philosopher and consultant.

His nonfiction books emphasize a systemic, holistic, cross-cultural and interdisciplinary perspective, while his fiction works and short stories focus upon education, philosophy, perennial wisdom, and the poetic formulation of an integrative worldview.

Pierre is a German-French bilingual native speaker and writes English as his 4th language after German, Latin and French. He also reads source literature for his research works in Spanish, Italian, Portuguese, and Dutch. In addition, Pierre has notions of Thai, Khmer, Chinese, Japanese, and Vietnamese.

All of Pierre's books are hand-crafted and self-published, designed by the author. Pierre publishes via his Delaware company, Sirius-C Media Galaxy LLC, and under the imprints of IPUBLICA and SCM (Sirius-C Media).

The author's profits from this book are being donated to charity.

CONTENTS

INTRODUCTION

Violence Begins Inside

All violence begins inside.

This is an insight that is above all others. It is a way to solve the violence trap that has been overlooked by both science and religion. It is the insight that violence is a *projection of inner processes*.

My hypothesis is that all violence we see in the world is but our inner violence projected outside. Violence is an attitude to escape from facing life, from facing conflicts, contradictions, oppositions and all we do not really understand.

Religions and ideologies of whatever kind have gradually but decidedly got us on the wrong path. They have alienated us from our own inner wisdom which is understanding life in its *complexity*. This understanding is based upon *holistic perception*, a form of knowledge gathering that is characterized by our two brain hemispheres working in synch.

What happened was that humanity *hypertrophied* the left brain hemisphere, *yang* qualities, logical thought, reasoning and deductive processes, neglecting, downplaying or shunning the *yin* qualities of the right brain, associative thought, fantasy and inductive processes. More and more alienated from their *inner selves*, humans search for outside sense-givers in the form of organized religion and ideologies.

These organizations have in common that they claim authority to judge what is right and wrong. They replaced natural self-regulation by moralistic behavior norms. They repressed the individual and blessed the group and group pressure. Individual wisdom became marginalized and even persecuted. They established schools, engaged in *mass alphabetization and missionarism*, gradually undermining parental authority and more or less totally disregarding the individual creative continuum of each and every child.

Then, they began to slaughter those who knew better, the *native populations* and ethnic minorities who, through their historic struggle have gained more wisdom than most dominator societies.

They created the hero cult, a single male god they called *Yahweh*, patriarchy, male dominance and all the rest of it. This happened long before the division of the three religions Judaism, Islam and Christianity. It is part of our cultural heritage.

This culture cannot help us to find peace because it has never practiced peace. It has systematically bred violence through an *obsession for control* that is the result of its disregard for pleasure and permissiveness and its insane rejection of the female principle.

Peace comes with dialogue and understanding, not through persecution and control, with respecting nature and not through violating nature, with accepting differences, not through holy wars that are out to bring more standards, more uniformity and more stupidity for all.

What we really need cannot be brought about through outside action or revolution, but only, as Krishnamurti has clearly shown, through a 'psychological revolution' from inside.

All violence begins inside and is first of all a lack of inner communication, of inner dialogue.

Self-knowledge comes once we acknowledge the truth that all sense-givers, authority and powers cannot reveal us our inner nature and cannot change our inner landscape. It comes through abandoning all attachment to those outside authorities, through building trust in the self-regulating wisdom of nature, the wisdom of *all-that-is.*

As all violence is first of all inner violence, all world peace is created by inner peace that is gradually projected outward, in the form of wistful action, fruitful cooperation, healing and respectful dialogue.

This, in turn, brings about real solutions, true solutions, not the fake solutions that are brought about through so-called political action that is cunning and deceitful.

Once we see that evolution comes from inside, we might open up to relearn the vocabulary of love instead of engaging in the next holy state war against drugs, pedophiles, terrorists or other social poison containers and scapegoat groups.

VIOLENCE BEGINS INSIDE

—See Peter Fritz Walter, Natural Order: Thesis, Antithesis and Synthesis in Human Evolution (Essays on Law, Policy and Psychiatry, Vol. 6, 2018).

It is through seeing our own self-delusions, our own antisocial desires and hangups and our own inner violence that we gradually begin to clean up the mess inside and *begin to understand life through understanding our opposites.* This understanding might be painful once we abandon our inner drug addictions which are our thousand beliefs in technological progress, machismo, physical prowess, racial superiority and all of *I-am-better-than-you* philosophies.

This painful awakening is the beginning of wisdom, and the journey into a new and peaceful lifestyle. It is what brings about humility.

This attitude listens to our opponents instead of shouting or shooting them down, knowing that we have got a part of their worldview in us and that, thus, we can empathetically understand their inner and outer tragedies. And then, change can come about, also outside, peacefully and totally uncontrolled.

Chapter One

Love and Morality

The reason why I entitled this chapter 'Love and Morality' is that I am forever convinced that love is the original thing and that compulsive sex morality in the form of *moralism* is a perversion of love; it is the corruption of natural love into artificial morality that has got us on the violence trap, in the first place.

Once you see that, you will agree that the discussion of patriarchy-matriarchy is absolutely random. The root of violence is denial of nature however we may call this denial.

Alienation from nature and natural functions comes about through a hypertrophy of the intellect, the new brain, the rational mind, the left brain and language. It is equally random if this happened, on a timeline, five thousand years ago or if it happened, as some meteorologists believe, through a climatic shift that led to a desertification of those regions in the Middle East where we know patriarchy first originated from.

—See, for example, James DeMeo, Saharasia (1998).

All these phenomena are secondary; they are effects, and not causes.

It is of little ontological value to know why and how people turned away from nature, most of them not being conscious of their bias against nature.

Compared to the amount of research spent on such scarcely relevant issues, it is in my view of paramount importance to know what turning away from nature exactly results in and what it costs us, in terms of organically grown networks destroyed, human life destroyed, animal life destroyed and plant life destroyed, and what it costs us in terms of planetary ecology.

It will then be seen that all religions and political ideologies that are nature-hostile *will have to restitute to humanity the high price we are paying*, as a human race, for the immense destruction their misled policies and beliefs have caused collectively!

Indeed, I believe they have to be made responsible for the destruction of human potential and the many possibilities of human realization they have destroyed. And if they do not act upon this insight, there is only one solution: they have to be disposed of, and as soon as possible, and as completely as possible, not as a matter of iconoclasm, but as a measure of world-political sanity!

When we begin to think *functionally, holistically and systemically*, and in the way nature 'thinks,' we will see that we need neither religions nor political salvation in any form to expand human potential in hitherto unforeseen ways.

We will then comprehend that being united with nature and its wisdom implies a natural and free spirituality that is based upon knowledge, and not belief, and that needs no gods or saviors because it is naturally complete and whole.

When love is again love and not a split concept that came about by a schizoid thought structure, violence will by itself disappear, without grandiose international efforts to counter it, and without billions spent on prevention that are better spent to *feed the millions of hungry children worldwide* who are left at stake by our well-fed, well-groomed and well-churched politicians.

The present state of violence is the result of wrong relationships!

Extensive research on the roots of violence has been undertaken and yet, it seems to me, one factor in the etiology of violence remains overlooked by most researchers. I contend that *violence begins inside,* in the sense that when our inner team is in conflict, we are torn apart and begin to project the schizoid split upon our outside reality; the deficient, distorted or totally lacking relationship of the inner parts of the psyche to each other brings about strife and conflict equally in our outward relationships.

Abuse is the result of a *power vacuum* that comes about through a fixation or complex within the lower self and that acts as a compensation to suffering early in life. People who are in touch with their inner truth and who are liberated of culturally created fear blockages are able to realize greater personal and collective happiness than they could hitherto opt for. More and more, it should be possible to make responsible love choices for relations that are unusual or even tabooed by former moral laws that belonged to the collective supremacy of the Pisces era.

The slogan 'Live Your Love' that I have coined as a viable new love paradigm is deliberately contrasting with nonsensical ideological and religious doctrines. It is these doctrines and their coercive dogmatism that have heavily contributed to bring about the chaotic state of violence that we face today almost everywhere in the world. Overcoming the violence trap means people have to relearn getting in touch with their inner truth so that they are again able to realize their greater vision of happiness: this includes to relearn *making love choices* in accordance with a higher form of wisdom that cares about synergy, and mutual positive development, and that is little concerned, for example, with the age of the partners involved in the relation.

One of the main objectives I gained from thirty years of research is the urgent need to *redefine natural sexuality for all ages* both on an individual level, through healing abuse, and on a collective level, through social reform. Part of this endeavor is to unveil the roots of violence and abuse, on both a personal and a collective level. Among the main reasons for violence being the repression of natural body pleasure and free love between people of all ages in general, and the child's free sexual life in particular, my task was to retrace the wrong turn that humanity has taken since prehistory and to embed this truth in a cross-cultural perspective that is focused upon the importance of love as a major factor of human evolution, and against compulsive sex morality which is the major factor of human devolution in general, and the debasement of human sexuality, in particular.

The pioneering work of Dr. Wilhelm Reich (1897-1957) in this field of research is of paramount importance, which is why I am going to shortly recapitulate and explain the findings of Wilhelm Reich and the *science of orgonomy* he created.

—See more in detail Peter Fritz Walter, Wilhelm Reich and the Function of the Orgasm, Great Minds Series, Vol. 11, 2015/2017.

Furthermore, it will be shown in my research that the findings of Wilhelm Reich only update for the ignorant West a science tradition in the East that knows since millennia the details about what Reich called *orgonomy*.

The essential truth gained from years of research on the functional processes of life is that all parts of the psyche must be given a voice so that a *constructive inner dialogue* can be set up. I favor an *integrated approach* to the problem that has seven complementary perspectives:

- a psychological perspective

- a historical perspective

- an artistic perspective

- a pedagogical perspective

- a political perspective

- a humanitarian perspective

- a spiritual perspective

Part of this task was to show the role of *erotic attraction to children* as an important manifestation of human love as it develops naturally *as a compensation for lacking child-child sexual contact in our society* and the general widespread *emotional abuse of the child* in the patriarchal and feel-hostile culture. It is to be shown that the repression of those compensatory love functions disturbs the natural love orgonomy and creates violence and abuse.

My research showed that child abuse and violence against children is not brought about by so-called 'pedophilia' but in the contrary through the repression of our natural *pedoemotions*.

Abuse is ill-defined in our culture. It only considers the victim and not the abuser. However, the abuser is a victim in as much as the person he has victimized. For truly, nobody can be victimized who has not previously chosen *to act as victim* in a given situation.

The abuser is trapped by the victim's paradigm in as much as the victim is trapped by the abuser's power problem or hangup. Both attract each other and there is no abuse without mutual implicit consent about acting out the two sides of abuse, the active and the passive one.

Fighting abuse is therefore not a moral cause but must start from a rational, functional and two-sided view of the problem as an *entanglement situation* that is karmic and inherent in both parties' life matrixes. *Moral wars, by contrast, lead to more confusion, more destruction and more abuse.* For they do not tackle the roots of abuse that are the same roots as the roots of violence and of incest, but only are concerned with the reflects that such shortcomings produce on the surface of society. They are for that reason entirely ineffective and superficial.

A viable solution can only come from tedious study and observation of all the factors involved in abuse and those factors are for the most part unconscious entanglement patterns hidden in the psyches of both abusers and abused, energetic blockages that have locked the stream of life in one or the other way so that parasitic patterns came about.

There is an urgent need to change the reigning love-and-abuse paradigm so as to combat violence and bring about positive change for constructive new relationships that are based upon the *golden rule of conduct* as it is taught by sages since times immemorial, and that are respected by most peaceful native cultures. It is to be seen in what horrendous ways both clerical and politically fascist movements and leaders have since centuries tried to veil this essential truth and thus spread the *emotional plague* all over the globe.

After extensive research on mythology, particularly the writings of Joseph Campbell, I gradually figured how the present love-killing paradigm came about us from ancient times. I namely had asked the question how it was possible that the former *love-based world order* was completely overthrown and violently eradicated by a new world order that has *replaced love by morality* and natural care by obligatory and largely standardized family relations?

Historically, the transition from peaceful and life-affirming matriarchal fishing-farming cultures to violent and life-denying hunting-killing patriarchal cultures is of particular importance for the understanding of the present *hero culture* with its strong 'Puritan' life denial, its obsessive focus on child protection and its repression of natural emotions.

There are important political consequences of my research. The corner stones of my social reform strategy and legal policy are the implementation of permissive education together with the *complete abandonment of all age-of-consent laws* and their replacement by *emosexual counseling for all ages*, effected by trusted experts, while the police completely retreats from interfering in human love and intimacy, whatever the age of the mates, as long as mating is consenting and nonviolent.

These policy changes would without further do for complete change in all our thinking, living and behaving; wars and massacres would cease; slavery, in which form ever would naturally cease when people's emotions are in balance, and all efforts for countering sexual pathologies and perversions would focus on prevention, instead of punishment; related problems would be handled in a no-nonsense, peaceful, professional and non-punitive manner that is effective socially and that involves *therapeutic and love-based spontaneous help*, instead of police intervention and the disruption of family bonds.

Most of these problems originate in *system-prone dysfunctions* that in the present legal system are inflated, like the disappearance of the extended family and the widespread acceptance of a neurotic, dysfunctional and insane family concept known as the 'nuclear family.'

I believe that there are important humanitarian consequences of my research. Special care must be bestowed upon children who can still be reformed and healed from biopathic deformations and characterological armors. There are millions of orphans to be found in state institutions all over the world. If only a small percentage could be taken care of in collaborating with responsible institutions that understand and support the need for permissiveness in education and the intelligent understanding of human emotions, humanity would be helped as a whole and true evolution would be possible.

The spiritual or religious impact of my concept of social and legal reform is obvious. It would lead humanity back to divine origins, through reconnecting us with our higher self. As long as humans are ruthlessly conditioned to comply with the often unreasonable and irrational demands of religions and ideologies, they cannot connect with their higher selves because they are torn up by either-or choices and by an unruly inner controller that drives them into restless and rushy behavior, which is shallow and superficial, keeping them in a state of constant aloofness that results form their alienation from natural inner guidance.

This is true for all involved, the children, the educators and all those who help building this new educational system. Negatively put, any attempt to change the dysfunctions and reduce violence in any given society *without attempting to change the educational system* will always be a ridiculous fake-solution that is based upon eye-wiping and 'quick fix' thinking.

Our educational system needs urgent and thorough reform and the relationships collective-individual, and state-individual need to be redefined; these areas have to be freed from the moralistic roof structure that keeps these vital areas of human living in a state of dysfunctionality and stagnation, which is in no way justifiable by any true and genuine morality. In the contrary, true morality goes along with *responsibility*, and to deny or obstruct change in the present catastrophic state of the world means to contribute to the rise of evil through the denial of responsibility, individual and collective.

CHAPTER TWO

The Value of Permissiveness

My hypothesis is that the destructiveness of civilization is the *result of the repression of the natural emotions of the child and the building of a moralistic roof structure* that gradually replaced the primary self-regulatory processes that nature has coded into the growth of all living.

Violence and destruction that characterize human history have their roots not in a biological or genetic error, but in the failure of civilization to keep in touch with nature's wisdom; this is mainly done by perverting children into obedient robots who have repressed their feelings in order to survive and to be accepted. To express it in a slogan, not civilization is wrong, but a civilization that *civilizes against nature.*

As examples to the contrary, I shall have a regard on tribal cultures, the pre-patriarchal high cultures of

Antiquity and some cultures that survived until today, as for example the Balinese culture, and where people are emotionally balanced, happy and productive, loyal and intelligent.

I already mentioned the highly developed *Minoan Civilization* with its natural focus on art, the senses and beauty, free sexuality and a matriarchal worldview that respected the female. This culture excelled with a low crime rate, absence of slavery, equality of women, a goddess cult and low level of violence. I also mentioned that crime rates in those cultures, if we take only the Balinese culture as an example, are relatively low, and violent crime such as murder and rape, abduction, rape and killing of children, is as good as non-existing. Marriages are long-lasting and divorce rates are considerably lower than in modern industrial cultures. These native cultures are more matriarchal in character than our highly violent modern civilizations which are predominantly patriarchal.

History reveals that already the first highly developed cultures, such as ancient Sumer, Babylon and the Maya and the Inca civilizations were belonging to the 'solar' patriarchal system. With patriarchy began the oppression of women and children and the reduction of sexuality toward certain sexual 'acts' that were allowed and certain other sexual 'acts' that were prohibited. With the increase of power for the patriarchal system, repression, denunciation, intolerance and structural, political, collective, domestic and intimacy violence began to reign where before freedom, peace, sexual permissiveness and tolerance were blooming.

An important factor within this process that keeps worsening until today is the repression of the child's natural emotions and sexual life.

As early as in 1929, Bronislaw Malinowski, a renowned anthropologist, published his report on the sexual life of the Trobriands in which he draws the reader's attention particularly to the sexual life of children and adolescents.

—See Bronislaw Malinowski, Sex and Repression in Savage Society (1927) and The Sexual Life of Savages in North West Melanesia (1929).

Malinowski found high sexual permissiveness toward children's free sexual play. More generally, he noted the total absence of a morality that condemns sexuality in children.

—Bronislaw Malinowski, Sex and Repression in Savage Society (1927), p. 76.

Malinowski observed that children engage in free sexual play from early age through a peculiar social institution. In fact, Malinowski found Trobriands maintain special houses for children and the youth, where the children, from age three, spend their nights, and where they gradually are initiated by older children in all forms of sexual play and later also coitus. Upon further inquiry, Malinowski learnt that the relations children maintain in these houses are meant to be promiscuous. He was told that Trobriands think that children should live out their inborn sexual drive in promiscuity in order to be able, after puberty, to form steady and stable relationships with a partner for marriage.

—See Bronislaw Malinowski, Sex and Repression in Savage Society (1927) and The Sexual Life of Savages in North West Melanesia (1929) as well as Margaret Mead, Sex and Temperament in Three Primitive Society (1935).

Notably, initiatory rites are absent with the Trobriands since children are initiated from about three years onwards, generally by older children, in all forms of sexual play. Interestingly, the Trobriand culture thus differs from most other tribal cultures in that there is very little stress upon the importance of adolescence or initiation rites for growing into adulthood.

With the Trobriands, who probably have the *phylogenetically more archaic social system* compared to most other tribal societies, adolescence is smooth and gradual, without any kind of revolt. The only marked difference of adolescence compared to childhood, in Trobriand is, as Malinowski reported, that originally promiscuous sexual behavior gradually transforms, during adolescence, into stable and non-promiscuous love relations, that seemingly prepare the young boys and girls for their later monogamous marriage.

The most interesting finding for Malinowski was that in Trobriand culture *violence is as good as non-existing* and that there are no sexual dysfunctions. To say, Trobriands were found to be almost ideal marriage partners and divorce was statistically under five percent, and thus a rare exception. Violent crimes are virtually non-existent and incest is tabooed and inhibited by social norms.

In his book *The Invasion of Compulsory Sex-Morality (1932/1971)*, Wilhelm Reich quoted extensively from Malinowski's field studies and used them for corroborating his own sex-economic theories. Other researchers found a similar social setup with the Muria in South India where children stay until their maturity in so-called *ghotuls* where they live their sexuality freely and in utter promiscuity, and where older children initiate younger ones progressively into sexual play.

—V. Elwin, The Muria and their Ghotul (1947), Richard L. Currier, Juvenile Sexuality in Global Perspective (1981).

These researchers found that after a phase of total promiscuity, the children, from the moment of sexual maturity, begin to form strong, stable and rather lasting bonds and partnerships which are based not on a desire for sexual adventure, but on love, and care. Research further found that these first steady relationships form the basis for later marriages that, regularly, last lifelong. (Id.)

Cultures with a matrilineal setup *raise children within their natural continuum balance* whereas patrilineal cultures tend to condition children according to firm cultural or ideological values and a rigid morality codex.

This ideological and religious conditioning that alienates the child from nature and from the natural functions of their body is primarily effected through indoctrination and through gradually alienating children from their bodies. The most effective way used to indoctrinate children with cultural prohibitions and taboos proceeds by implanting early in them a *deeply rooted doubt about who they are!* This doubt which creates a vacuum will then be filled with magic formulas such as *Be not what you are!* The next step is to force the child to play roles in order to please their parents. The main role in this drama which is the *Drama of the Gifted Child (1996)*, as Alice Miller called her book, is the role of the child as father or mother of his own narcissistic parents.

This education that I describe with the formula 'rearing narcissistic comedians' is very common in our postmodern industrial culture. This is why *narcissism*, a serious emotional affliction, is rampant in all our modern democracies. However, few researchers are able to look through the cultural veil and see the roots of narcissism where they are, namely in our child rearing paradigm.

Those who do, such as Alice Miller or Alexander Lowen are not representing mainstream psychiatry, despite the brilliance of their work.

—See, for example, Alice Miller, Thou Shalt Not Be Aware (1998), Alexander Lowen, Narcissism (1997).

They have found that education that typically leads to narcissism is rich in inventing and executing several other magic formulas that are given to the child as 'hypnotic spells.' Some of these are:

- Be adaptable and flexible until self-alienation

- Never be yourself in front of your parents

- Be not child-like

- Be mature in immaturity

- Understand what your parents don't understand

- Be logical and uncomplicated

- ▸ Respect your parents while disregarding yourself

- ▸ Mistrust your intuition

- ▸ Follow authority without questioning

Many parents who educate their children in a system-conform manner are not conscious of the fact that they act as the long arm of political systems and ideologies subtly hypnotizing their children with the concepts they have themselves been fed with.

Education toward autonomy is based upon the unique truth of every single child, also and especially if this individual truth is totally contrary to the reigning sociopolitical ideologies.

It is disturbing for industrial culture that the child be a complete sexual being from birth, and that, as a result, children have a birthright to have their emotions and their sexual feelings respected. Françoise Dolto wrote in her book *La Cause des Enfants (1985)* that it scandalizes adults that a child be their equal and that, therefore, most parents raise their children as formerly princes ruled their kingdoms.

The sociopolitical reasons why this is so are obvious: a body-oriented child is not a consumer of toys and a thousand devices artificially created by industrial culture.

For those who object this view, I recall that the repression of the child's sexuality has started precisely with the onset of the Western industrial bourgeoisie, at the end of the 17th century.

—Françoise Dolto, La Cause des Enfants (1985), pp. 28-29.

Historical studies about child rearing practices in Europe stress the fact that still during the Renaissance the sexuality of the child was not interfered with, and that, back in the Middle-Ages, apart from Christian circles, it was completely free.

Consumerist industrialization brought the societal replacement of body pleasure or a state of *To Be* by ersatz body pleasure, or a state of *To Have*, to quote Erich Fromm's terminology.

—Erich Fromm, To Have or To Be (1976/1996).

Ersatz body pleasure is the pleasure that replaces original body pleasure; thus first of all the toy. Not the self-made toy that still has some connection with the body, but the industrially produced toy that is completely alien to the child's body. Typically this toy —which in the meantime is produced by a gigantic worldwide industry—consists of materials not akin to the human body, such as *plastic* and *metal*.

Both materials have in common that they are cold and rigid while the body is warm and pliable. Unconsciously children are conditioned upon the characteristics of the toys they is playing with. *Be plastic!* translates into *Be without feelings, artificial. Be metal!* translates into *Be hard and mechanical.* These are the characteristics of the culture you are growing into. So mold yourself accordingly!

In addition, techniques of confusion are used in education to gradually alienate the child from their own truth—which is their body continuum. The child namely thinks from the body toward the mind, and thus *inductively* while the conditioned adult thinks from the mind toward the body, that is *deductively.* This means that the child's truth is defined and experienced as the *truth of their body.* Every truth that disregards this body or tries to set it aside will not be regarded by the child as truth.

It is for this reason that children *cannot comprehend morality* and moralistic educational concepts as those concepts deny the body and are to be understood only by the rational mind. The result are water-headed giant babies, adults who have never made the cut with their childhood and that remain erotically immature. True virgins.

But life has not made us to remain virgins, but to leave virginity and grow into loving copulation— otherwise life could not continue.

CHAPTER THREE

Pleasure Defeats Violence

Herbert James Campbell, a renowned English neurologist, found in two decades of research a universal principle which controls our brain and that he called the *pleasure principle*. His book *The Pleasure Areas (1973)* provides a summary of many years of neurological research. Campbell shows in his extensive study that our entire thinking and living is primarily motivated by pleasure, pleasure not only as tactile, sensuous or sexual sensation, but also as non-sensuous, intellectual or spiritual pleasure.

With these findings, the old theoretical controversy if man was primarily a biological or a spiritual being, became obsolete; it is our striving for pleasure that induces certain interests in us, that drives us to certain actions and that lets us choose certain ways.

During childhood and depending on the outside stimuli, certain preferred pathways are traced in our brain, which means that *specific neural connections* are established that serve the information flow. The number of those connections is namely an indicator for intelligence. The more *preferred pathways* exist in the brain of a person, the more lively appears the person, the more interested she will be in different things, and the quicker she will achieve integrating new knowledge into existing memory.

High memorization ability, Campbell found, is namely depending on how easily new information can be added to existing pathways of information. Logically, the more of those pathways there are in the brain, the better! Many preferred pathways make for high flexibility and the capacity to adapt easily to new circumstances.

Campbell's research indicates that the repression of pleasure that is since centuries part of our Judeo-Christian culture, has strongly impeded evolution and impaired the integrity of the human psyche and health. This is exactly what Wilhelm Reich found – without having at his disposition Campbell's new neurological findings.

But not only neurologists such as Campbell have nowadays thought about the basic functions of life and living, but also people who were formerly active in totally different fields of science. The American scientists Ashley Montagu and James W. Prescott had very different points of departure for their extensive research. Montagu wanted to know why in animal experiments small rhesus apes died when they were deprived from their mother while they survived when a simple felt mat was put in the cage as surrogate of motherly tactile affection.

Prescott researched the origins of violence, and the *relationship between pleasure and violence*. He was from the start skeptical regarding the age-old myth that man was per se a violent creature even though human history, or what historians saw of it, seemed to prove this assumption. Both scientists came to basically the same results, namely that tactile stimulation of the infant as a main source of early pleasure gratification is the primary condition for human health, for harmony, and for world peace.

Ashley Montagu's research developed quickly a specific focus on the importance of the *human skin* as a prime pleasure provider. *Grant's Method of*

Anatomy (1980) defines the skin as the most extended and the most varied of our sensory organs. Ashley Montagu's study *Touching: The Human Significance of the Skin (1971)* is the final result of decades of skin research, not only Montagu's, but of many other researchers whose findings Montagu summarizes and evaluates in his extensive study.

This research elucidates the importance of tactile stimulation in early childhood. Montagu's specific focus in his research was upon the mammal mothers' licking the young. He found astonishing unity in zoologists' opinions as to the importance of motherly licking for the survival of the young. Montagu namely discovered that it was in the first place the *perineal zone,* the region between anus and genitals, of the young animals that the mother preferably and repeatedly licked.

Experiments in which mammal mothers were impeded from licking this zone of the young resulted in functional disturbances or even chronic sickness of the genito-urinary tract of the young animals. Montagu concluded from his research that the licking did not serve hygienic purposes only, but was intended to provide a tactile stimulation for the organs that were underlying the part of the skin that was licked. (Id., pp. 15 ff.)

Montagu further concluded that licking rarely happens in the mother-child relationship with primates or humans. (Id., p. 18) Most researchers found that during evolution, *licking was gradually replaced by eye or skin contact* between mother and child. The tactile needs of the small child correspond to the desire of the parents to express love through tactile affection such as kissing or fondling, pressing the child's naked body against one's own during play hour, and the naked co-sleeping of parents and children, which is something very common with Eskimos and other tribal cultures.

In the run of industrial civilization, however, this changed fundamentally. Modern pediatrics or child psychologists recommend parents to put their children in separate rooms and beds with the result that parents and children are physically separated. The civilized child gets much less tactile stimulation in early childhood than children from most tribal cultures, a fact that was observed even by casual observants of native lifestyle, such as Jean Liedloff, a cinematographer and author of a revealing study on the tactile needs of infants. Liedloff also is credited with having coined the expression *Continuum Concept*, title of her book, that has been accepted by most of postmodern anthropological and psychological research on *early tactile deprivation.*

—Jean Liedloff, The Continuum Concept (1977).

Ashley Montagu and James W. Prescott, coming from different scientific angles, concluded as to the *importance of early tactile stimulation for the psychic and physical health of the child.*

A direct relationship was discovered by both between early tactile stimulation and the functioning of the immune system of the child. The relationship was corroborated by France's first and foremost obstetricians, Frederick Leboyer and Michel Odent. As Michel Odent writes in his book *La Santé Primale (1986):*

> It is not yet completely understood that sensorial perceptions at the beginning of life can be a way to stimulate the 'primary brain,' at a time when the 'system of primary adaptation' is not yet grown to maturity. More specifically, this signifies for example that, if one fondles a human baby or an animal baby, one also stimulates his immune system. (Id., p. 24, Translation mine)

Montagu states in his book that love was once defined as the 'harmony of two souls and the contact of two epidermises.' In this sense the *peau à peau* that is now recommended to mothers by their pediatricians, is indeed a *primary condition* for the healthy growing up of children, the good functioning of their immune system and, last not least, the early creation of preferred pathways in their brains.

Abundant skin contact thus favors high intelligence!

In his research with rhesus, Montagu came to astonishing findings. When he deprived the newborns of their mother and put them in a 'naked' cage, they died. When he did the same, but put a kind of felt mat in the cage, they survived, although they carried away some brain damage from the deprivation of the mother. However, it was a fact that the 'felt mat' assured their survival.

How could that be? Montagu went one step further. He replaced the mother through a 'felt mother' that was hung in the cage. Now the young did not only survive but they also had almost no more brain damage. It was especially the first part of the experiment that intrigued Montagu, that the young survived simply by the fact that a felt mat was put in the cage. Further observations led Montagu to see that the young rhesus used the 'carpet' creatively for giving to their bodies tactile stimulation, which obviously served as a compensate for the tactile stimulation they normally got from their mother in the form of licking.

The interesting thing about this experiment is that it was not the milk of the mother nor her care that was essential for the young's survival, but exclusively her *providing some form of tactile pleasure*. The felt of the carpet was similar to the mother's fur and therefore acceptable for the young as a mother surrogate. This research amply demonstrates the *importance of tactile stimulation with all mammals*, and so much the more with humans where primary symbiosis is even more prolonged!

Already in the 1930s Wilhelm Reich disproved the widespread misconception that sadistic and destructive tendencies were part of human nature. He namely opposed Sigmund Freud and his theory of a *death instinct,* demonstrating through biogenic research that those assumed destructive instincts are but *secondary drives*, a direct consequence of the cultural repression of the natural sexual instinct which had brought about a collective neurosis in the human animal. Reich's insights that at his lifetime were violently opposed by the majority of his scientific colleagues, now are confirmed by Prescott's findings which bring statistic evidence as to the malleability of the human individual through his early tactile experiences or the absence of such experiences.

Prescott, using R.B. Textor's supra-cultural statistics published in *A Cross-Cultural Summery (1967)* to scientifically prove his highly explosive political conclusions, writes:

> Unless the causes of violence are isolated and treated, we will continue to live in a world of fear and apprehension. Unfortunately, violence is often offered as a solution to violence. Many law enforcement officials advocate 'get tough' policies as the best method to reduce crime. Imprisoning people, our usual way of dealing with crime, will not solve the problem, because the causes of violence lie in our basic values and the way in which we bring up our children and youth. Physical punishment, violent films and TV programs teach our children that physical violence is normal. (…) Recent research supports the point of view that the deprivation of physical pleasure is a major ingredient in the expression of physical violence.

The common association of sex with violence provides a clue to understanding physical violence in terms of deprivation of physical pleasure. (...) Although physical pleasure and physical violence seem worlds apart, there seems to be a subtle and intimate connection between the two. Until the relationship between pleasure and violence is understood, violence will continue to escalate.

—James W. Prescott, Body Pleasure and the Origins of Violence, Bulletin of the Atomic Scientists, 10-20 (1975), partly reprinted in: The Futurist, April, 1975, pp. 10-11.

Prescott thus fully confirmed Reich's earlier research and corroborated his socioeconomic and sex-economic findings. More specifically, he found a remarkable relationship between pleasure and violence. Referring to laboratory experiments with animals, Prescott could detect a sort of reciprocal relationship between pleasure and violence, that is *the presence of pleasure inhibits violence*—and *vice versa*. (Id., p. 10)

Furthermore, Prescott found a direct relationship between the child rearing methods of a given culture, and the degree of violence that reigns in that culture. In detail, he found that societies that tend to rear children in a rather Spartan way, hostile to pleasure and with little or no tactile stimulation, commit in their value system to various forms of violence, do warfare, torture their enemies, practice slavery and progeny and concede to women and children a rather low social status; these societies also exhibit a high crime rate. (Id., p. 12)

Another violence-indicating parameter in a society, Prescott found, is physical violence towards children in form of corporal punishment. (Id.)

Furthermore, repression or tolerance of children's sexual life plays a decisive role in the assessment if a given society has a high or low violence potential. Prescott elucidates:

> Thus, we seem to have a firmly based principle: Physically affectionate human societies are highly unlikely to be physically violent. Accordingly, when physical affection and pleasure during adolescence as well as infancy are related to measures of violence, we find direct evidence of a *significant relationship between the punishment of premarital sex behaviors and various measures of crime and violence.* (Id., p. 13)

As a result of his extensive research, Dr. Prescott advocates the abolition of corporal punishment of children, a definite social and legal rise of the social status of women, the reinstitution of the extended family, the reintegration of the elder and a the active participation of men with child rearing and the granting of physical affection to children in their role as fathers or educators.

—See James W. Prescott, Deprivation of Physical Affection as a Primary Process in the Development of Physical Violence (1979), pp. 77, 78.

I discovered the writings of James W. Prescott, PhD in the 1980s, at a time when I was doing research on Ashley Montagu, Frederick Leboyer, Michel Odent, Alexander Lowen, Bronislaw Malinowski, and Margaret Mead. The two major articles written by James W. Prescott were coming to me like a revelation to a question I had asked since more than a decade: 'What are the roots of violence?'

Knowing from anthropological, ethnological, and sociological studies as well as from neuropsychology and from spiritual work that violence is not the natural condition for humanity, but a sort of emotional and cultural perversion that results from deep hurts early in childhood, and probably also from scars that go back to former lives, I was grateful to have found at last conclusive research that not only analyzed our condition, but also pointed to viable long-term solutions for creating a more peaceful society of the future.

Prescott's research also integrates findings by lesser known researchers as Dr. Harlow who have focused on the brain development of rhesus, and who found revealing evidence for the fact that among all the factors that make a mammal infant survive without the mother, the *one single essential factor is the availability of a 'touchable' object that provides tactile stimulation.*

For example, in a widely documented experiment, two mother surrogates were hung in the cage, one serving as a milk provider, the other being a soft doll made from linen. The surprising thing was that all rhesus infants preferred the *cloth mother* over the milk-giving mother, thereby signaling that tactile stimulation was the most important in their parenting needs, not the secondary availability of mother milk.

Today, this research has been corroborated by newer brain research, conducted by a variety of researchers starting with Herbert James Campbell in the 1970s, and with James W. Prescott as the expert who shows in a number of publications that tactile stimulation of infants together with breastfeeding and baby-carrying are the most important factors for building nonviolent, socially positive and non-abusive behaviors.

To repeat it, the solutions that James W. Prescott suggests are long-overdue changes in the process of childbirth and our educational system, permissive and nonviolent child-rearing together with greater social permissiveness for premarital sex and a definite legal prohibition of physical punishment of children in both the home and school together with effective government collaboration for fighting domestic, educational and sexual violence.

Regarding infant care, Prescott stresses the importance of the *primary symbiosis* between mother and infant during the first 18 months of the infant, abundant tactile stimulation of infants and babies, using techniques of child massage, as well as co-sleeping between parents and small children.

Another important field of research that could be classified under the header of 'ritual violence' is both male circumcision and the widespread genital mutilation of female infants, girls and women, which is now discussed under the header of 'female genital cutting' or FGC. James W. Prescott advocates the complete abandonment of such practices that I heard about first in 1984, when doing a legal research on the matter for Edmond Kaiser, founder of *Terre des Hommes* in Lausanne, Switzerland. At the time I thought these violent practices were limited to some communities in Somalia, Sudan and other African countries, but fact is that it's a worldwide problem.

The *American Academy of Pediatrics* writes in their policy statement that it was estimated that 'at least 100 million women have undergone FGC and that between 4 and 5 million procedures are performed annually on female infants and children, with the most severe types performed in Somalian and Sudanese populations.'

> —American Academy of Pediatrics, Policy Statement—Ritual Genital Cutting of Female Minors, http://pediatrics.aappublications.org/cgi/content/full/125/5/1088.

In addition, what is lesser known is the fact, reported by the American Academy of Pediatrics that these practices are not limited to Muslim populations but are known also from orthodox circles among Christians and Jews. (Id.)

The perhaps most important research topic where James W. Prescott is widely recognized as an expert is violence prevention. He particularly stresses the importance of breastfeeding-bonding for 2.5 years or longer. He emphasizes that nonviolent behaviors develop as a result of cognitive affectional bonding between mother and infant.

Together with a number of other researchers, he has recently documented and published scientific evidence that shows beyond doubt that the human brain develops differently in humans who as infants have enjoyed prolonged breastfeeding, and in those who have not.

It is interesting to note that the suggestions that James W. Prescott comes up with from his perspective as a peace researcher are very much in accordance with those suggested by Jean Liedloff, in her book *The Continuum Concept (1977)*, from her perspective of the lifestyle of native peoples.

Also, there is a striking similarity of solutions offered for the same questions by Ashley Montagu, as a result of skin research, and by the French obstetricians Michel Odent and Frederick Leboyer who have looked beyond the fence of obstetrics and into what Odent called *Primal Health,* which is a holistic concept of health and wellbeing.

In my perspective and the overview I had over Prescott's research, it seems to me that the central focus is the preparation of far-reaching policy changes for the political agenda that are backed up by hard scientific data. In so far, I consider Prescott as a researcher more important than many others who are perhaps more published and more famous than him. In fact, the importance of his research can hardly be underestimated. We are living wrongly as a society and the violence we face is not hazard, nor a 'biological mistake' but the precise result of our living against the wisdom of nature.

Research in neuroscience delivers the clear-cut evidence that touch is paramount for the development of nonviolent and socially positive behaviors. Dr. Prescott shows that sensory deprivation results in behavioral abnormalities such as depression, impulse dyscontrol, violence, substance abuse, and in impaired immunological functioning in mother deprived infants. He demonstrated through a research with 49 native cultures that there are precise correlations between *low affectionate cultures, insufficient mother-infant bonding, patrilinearity, polygeny, warfare, slavery, torture of enemies, sexual repression, child abuse, violence and monotheism,* on the one hand, and *high affectionate cultures, nurturant mother-infant bonding, matrilinearity, low polygeny rate, absence of warfare, no slavery and no torture, sexual permissiveness, high infant indulgence, peaceful coexistence and polytheism.*

To summarize, Prescott's research sees the primary problem in the etiology of violence in failed bonding in the mother-infant relationship and so-called somato-sensory affectional deprivation (S-SAD), as such deprivation causes developmental brain abnormalities. The brain that results from this abnormal upbringing is the *NeuroDissociative Brain.*

It is related to *pain, theistic religions, gender inequality, sexual puritanism, addictive synthetic drugs, authoritarian control, depression, violence, warfare, a biomedical health model, and politics of betrayal.* The healthy brain, which develops when affectional cognitive bonding between mother and infant was nurturant and adequate, is able to experience pleasure. It is related to *earth religions, is matrilineal and favors gender equality, sexual liberty, natural botanical drugs, egalitarian freedom, a biobehavioral health model and politics of trust.*

It is important to realize that we have not one single factor here, but a whole *pattern of factors* that belong as it were together.

This is exactly what I emphasized in my own research on the *Eight Dynamic Patterns of Living* where I show that most native cultures that are allowing to build the limbic-subcortical emotional brain through adequate parenting are favoring eight patterns of living in their overall lifestyle, which are autonomy, ecstasy, energy, language, love, pleasure, self-regulation and touch.

—See Peter Fritz Walter, Eight Dynamic Patterns of Living: Base Elements of True Civilization (Essays on Law, Policy & Psychiatry, Vol. 2, 2018).

CHAPTER FOUR

Breaking the Vicious Circle

The research outlined here so far should suffice for a first assessment of the 'impossible human' that governments around the world, and their police forces, target for 'improvement,' and 'social education.' Their attempts are obviously fighting violence with violence, evil with evil, and socially sanctified schizophrenia with legalized paranoia.

When many researchers, from very different scientific angles, come to the result that not the human is bad, but how the human is educated and distorted in early childhood, and how natural love is thwarted through the rather perverse idea of compulsive morality, then we have to question the base assumption behind our whole legally incensed altar of violent moralism!

The base assumption in this system namely is that the human is *originally bad and corrupt,* or has been rendered so by 'original sin' or its worldly correlate, the so-called 'hereditary hangup.'

The first idea, favored by our major monotheistic religions, says 'Human is born evil but can be redeemed by our Great Religion,' the second variant, now fashionable in the 'science society' says 'Human is born with hereditary defect and can be repaired by our Great Psychiatry.' It's exactly the same mechanistic and nonsensical idea, only that the vocabulary changed.

Neither our great religions nor our great psychiatry obviously have understood that the human being is without fault, but that the mold the human is baked in roots out the last little rest of good, by distorting our perception early in life, and by *blocking our natural emotional flow* through the worldwide plague of moralism, that is the blasphemic and deeply nature-hostile idea that there was something fundamentally wrong with the human setup.

What is wrong here is that our worldwide religious and political power conglomerates have an interest in upholding the myth of the 'impossible human' for their politics of *divide et impera*, their relentless flow of income from all wars, civil wars and rampant genocide of tribal populations, and their dominion over the world banking system.

It is easy, when you are a doctor, telling your patients how sick they are, to inflate your doctor's bills. It is easy when you are a pharmacist, telling your clients how bad their doctor is, to inflate your pharmacist's bills. It is easy when you are a psychiatrist, to tell your clients how insignificant the body is, and that's the human mind that is the big culprit in human history, to inflate your psychiatrist's bills. It is easy, when you are a lawyer, to tell your clients how helpless doctors, pharmacists and psychiatrists are in the face of the *single valid reality* that every human is a criminal by birth, to inflate your lawyer's bills. It is easy, when you are a politician, to tell your voters that doctors, pharmacists, psychiatrists and lawyers are all bad advisors as only politics can change the impossible human in the long run, to inflate your politician's budget. It is easy when you are a holy man, to tell your disciples how ignorant doctors, pharmacists, psychiatrists, lawyers and politicians are of spiritual reality, to inflate your good karma.

All these people have an interest to tell you how bad you are, what a bad karma you have, what a bad karma your society has or your nation, and how hopeless the overall situation is for our planet to survive global warming and all the rest of cataclysms that are going to rain upon us and plague us like the proverbial Pandorabox.

Are you not bombarded every day with catastrophic messages that are not per se catastrophic but become so because they are *inflated by the modern mass media* and the fact that all is networked for telling you that on the other side of the globe a woman was raped, a child was abused and a man had sex with his small daughter, while the world strangely enough is not networked for telling you what improvements were made, and how happy people are in their families, compared to the misery of togetherness you are in since twenty-five years and that you call 'my marriage'?

And what you are never told is how abysmal the situation is in your *glorious democracy* for those who are unable to handle the bioenergy contained in their emotions, and who are jailed for years, if not for decades, for having taken so-called *drugs*, engaged in the wrong kind of sex with the wrong kind of person or killed a neurotic, dominant, oppressive or abusive mother or spouse!? This reality is carefully veiled from you so that you continue to believe how well off you are in your particular reality soup that is largely brewed not by yourself, but by those on top of the media hierarchy.

Have you ever seen how a prison cell looks from inside, and how cruelly children are beaten in so-called 'correction homes' which are jails for children for which your government, in whatever country you live, has till this day not enacted the anti-torture conventions and human rights precepts because *they are valid only for adults, and for prisons that keep adults.*

Children, sorry, are not legally valid consumers, which is shown very clearly by the fact that their consent to sexual embrace with adults is 'deemed legally invalid'. So if these young members of our society are jailed, they can be treated in any possible way because nobody will feel responsible, their parents having been discredited as 'abusers' or otherwise declared unable for caretaking, and the government doing what is prescribed by the laws. And the laws, sorry, have forgotten to enact any of our *glorious human rights protection instruments* and conventions for our smallest members; and our child protection laws target abusive parents and of course the proverbial stranger-rapist, but not abusive governments!

This is a little snapshot from the behind-the-stage of your magnificent democracy, but you prefer to read what's hot in your news, right? And you think that on top of this mess of brutality, ignorance, and confusion of values, you are going to establish world peace? One must be struck with debility to believe that, really.

So, when you see that, you see *all*, namely the fact that before we can even *think* of peace for this globe, we have to clean up the mess inside of our minds and behind-the-stage.

The truth is that you are *not born in sin*, that you are not born in destructive karma as a predestined fate, that you do not need to be 'professionally' treated for being acceptable for society, nor 'religiously' treated for being acceptable to the otherworld. The truth is that you are a complete god when, and as long as, you are a complete human!

You don't need to imitate heroes and avatars, for they were and are just that, complete humans. The hero is like you, only that their message and expression are tailored to their individual mission. There is no high and low among humans. You have all within you that you see in your favorite heroes but god manifests through you in a different way than the supreme spirit manifests through this or that hero, and that is why you are important for creation.

If you were like the heroes you admire, the supreme highest spirit could not manifest through you because you are created for manifesting a particular *Gestalt* of spiritual truth, which is expressing itself through your particular life's mission. Therefore, you are important *as you are* and you are less important as long as you feel compelled to imitate others. In fact, if you mold yourself into the image of your cherished hero, you are useless for the universal mind to manifest spiritual truth through you. Affirm this truth over and over:

Infinite Spirit in its Wisdom opens up the Gateway for My True Expression in Life and Guides Me

Every Day in Perfect Health, Happiness and Prosperity!

You don't need doctors, spiritual advisors, gurus or healers. You can heal yourself. There is a simple method to heal early trauma; you don't need self-hypnosis, and expensive therapies. You have the gift of expressing yourself through writing. Write the simple truth.

The simple truth is how you have lived your childhood, how you have experienced your early life. You do this without judging, without positive or negative, without inflicting a good-or-bad judgment on each episode, anecdote or experience in your childhood. You simply say and write how you felt it. This is how you are going to heal your inner wounds, namely through seeing yourself, and your life, objectively, without adding on and without leaving out details. This self-healing is part of your spiritual perfection as a complete human.

Breaking the vicious circle of violence, there is only one way, focus upon love, undivided, unspoiled, unconditional love, which is not passion, not desire, not entanglement, but freedom and respect of the other as a god-manifesting creature, just as yourself.

When you realize this, you see that violence in the world is the violence in us projected upon the world, and that for fighting violence, we have to find a way to end our inner violence, our inner strife and turmoil, which is brought about through the many contradictions we are in, and through the oppression inflicted upon us by a society that hasn't really done an evolution since the last five thousand years, in that it remained stuck in insignificant technological progress while psychologically being on the level of the primal horde.

CHAPTER FIVE

The Tactile Imperative

In this present chapter I direct my focus upon the real and possible human; we have seen that projecting upon the human being what in fact belongs to our cultural confusion is not a smart way to bring about peace.

We have the whole of written human history on the table to prove that doing this does not bring about peace, but war and destruction and large-scale misery. I would even go as far as saying that the problem perceived with 'sexual aggression' as one of the typical traits attributed to the 'impossible human' is contained in the very term of 'sex,' with its inherent confusion of sexual mating with sensuality and tactile stimulation.

The very fact of a *terminological split between love and sex* implies the possibility of a splitting off the sexual function from a loving give-and-take, so that love remains a kind of residual concept of 'pure caring and affection' which, of course, is sheer nonsense as it does not exist in life.

This form of *reductionism* is one of the ways that because of losing the original joy of living, the human began to intellectualize love, instead of living love.

—See Michel Odent, The Scientification of Love (1999).

This cultural schizoid split between 'love and sex' makes for a lot of damage in our striving for unity, coherence and harmony in relationships.

The reader may object that it often happens that sexuality is lived in its cold form, deprived of love, as mere satisfaction of desire and rather brutally, and that some people even experience more intense sexual feelings when they can encounter sex without being obliged to fake tenderness or caring.

This may be true. The ego trip may give you a strong discharge, but this proves only to what point you have been 'charged' prior to it, to what point you have been tense! In fact, research has shown that sex which is experienced connected with love, and where the sexual activity was motivated by love, not by an instinct for dominating and 'stabbing' the other sexually, engenders a higher level of lasting feelings of happiness and joy than sex that is acted out in the form of an ego-trip.

Whatever your personal opinion on this matter may be like, there is no doubt about the fact that sexuality in every form is focused upon our skin as the main sexual organ!

It seems, however, that sexology has only hesitantly taken the turn to consider the importance of *skin contact* in the give and take of body pleasure. As we have seen, deprivation of tactile pleasure creates a nasty misbalance in the psychosomatic setup of the child. Besides, licking, fondling and caressing all genital parts of the child's body with the lips and the tongue is a positive means of communicating to the child the importance of validating these erotic body parts as essentially sweet and beautiful.

This describes just one attitude of what today in alternative circles is called *sensuous parenting*, and that I consider as progressive and erotically intelligent.

This is one expression of how the possible human can live and act in alignment with nature, instead of fighting against nature. The skin is our primary sexual organ. All erotic stimulation of sexual organs is effected through the stimulation of the skin that surrounds them. Needless to add that this is not a cultural novelty, but is widely practiced in cultures like India, where mothers use to massage their infants, toddlers and children, which includes the gentle massage of their genital parts, as Frederick Leboyer reports it in his book *Loving Hands, The Traditional Art of Baby Massage (1977)*.

However, Sigmund Freud defined sexuality as any behavior that has a physical connotation to the sexual organs and that is focused on receiving pleasure. And here is where the cultural confusion starts. Why should we qualify caring parental behavior as 'sexual' only because it focuses on the child's genitals? When your son has a phimosis, and you gently massage the penis every day with body lotion to liberate the tight foreskin and render it smoother, for helping your child to avoid painful surgery, have you engaged in 'sex' with your child, have you been incestuous, have you 'abused' your child?

The very fact that *I need to ask these questions* shows to what point we are 'culturally confused' and how much Freudian 'psychoanalysis' confused us further. We should ask if body pleasure really must be concentrated on the sexual organs so that we can qualify it as sexual? It is certainly also a form of body pleasure to drink a fresh beer or to eat one's favorite dish. However, this kind of pleasure would more appropriately be called *oral* or *nutritive* pleasure. Hardly anyone would go as far as qualifying it as sexual. But how is it with caressing our loved one's chest or bottom? Is it sexual or not? Does it depend on the way we caress that it is sexual or merely affectionate, or does it depend on the intention? Or is the decisive factor which body zone is caressed? Or does it depend on the fact that the one who caresses is sexually aroused by the activity—or not? Still during the Renaissance it was common in Europe that all members of the family slept naked in one bed, as today it still is practiced with the Eskimo and many other native populations. The bodily touch or casual caresses that happened during the night were generally not considered as sexual or sexually intended.

Today, in our culture, many people would find it unusual to let sleep their children naked in one bed or that parents would sleep naked with their children in one bed. This is quite astonishing since the majority of scientists and psychologists are now outspoken about *children's need for direct body contact, warmth, togetherness, tenderness, nudity*—and this independently of age or gender!

Many scientists have researched on the consequences of a *deprivation of love nutrition* in the form of lacking tactile pleasure, and got alarming results. After the publication of volumes if not entire libraries of results of this research, now almost all specialists in early child care agree that children raised deprived of love, tenderness and caring body touch face greater adaptation problems later in life, frequently show learning difficulties and tend to be more rigid in experiencing joy and pleasure than children who grew up with love and body touch.

The first group of children exhibits symptoms such as restlessness or hyperactivity; in school they often have drawbacks because of their low attention span and concentration ability. In the group, they are seen as rather isolationist and uncooperative. They are easily pushed aside as 'difficult', and once this happens, the symptoms aggravate, sometimes dramatically. Most children in institutions for so-called 'delinquent youth' have been deprived of basic body touch and stimulation of their emotional intelligence; often an intolerant and punitive attitude from the side of the environment made them turn away from sociability and into marginality.

What is specifically pathological in their behavior and in the circumstances that have contributed to form it? How does it impact on children if in their family tenderness and care was replaced by violence and brutality? Research on domestic violence has shown that healthy forms of body touch and body pleasure do virtually not exist in such families! If there is touch at all, it is one that hurts, violates, humiliates and degrades.

There is unanimity among scientists and healthcare professionals that for the small child tactile stimulation is essential for its healthy psychosomatic growth. It has been shown that close and long-term body contact between the child and their mother or father, or other nutritive caretakers *decisively strengthens the child's immune system and improves their health.* One could conclude that these findings are not only valid for small children but also children between the age of six until puberty, and even adolescents, for what could be called skin erotics seems to be a life-enhancing and health-strengthening factor in all living.

In fact, in India, as Frederick Leboyer reports, where it is a common tradition to massage babies with warm oil, there are many mothers who continue massaging their children, which always includes gently massaging their genitals, until adolescence.

—See Frederick Leboyer, Loving Hands (1977).

It is believed in India that massaging children's genitals will enhance their procreative ability, sexual potency and resistance against illness. Such tactile forms of childcare are however by no means associated in India with incest or pedophilia simply because they are *not considered as sexual.*

They are instead regarded as a natural and necessary attribute to essentially nurturant parental care.

Chapter Six

The Birth of Functional Thinking

The possible human can only come about in alignment with nature, not against nature. And therefore, the possible human can only be a functional thinker; the impossible human was a dysfunctional thinker, as long namely as he was a moralist. *Nature is basically functional.*

There is no morality in nature and no need to establish one on top of nature. Life is good as it is. It's the *plague of moralism* that over centuries if not millennia has distorted human thinking into a mess of guilt-related and shame-related convolutions and inner contradictions that eventually brought about that amount of inner violence that we see projected upon life and that created all our wars and civil wars over the course of human history.

Moralistic thinking never is functional; the advocates of child protection cunningly veil this fact by drafting an agenda of social and political issues around *The Child* as a cult object, a fetish and an embodiment of puppet-values. Functional thinking follows nature's inherent logic; it fosters and supports growth, and is economical, using the least of effort to bring about a maximum effect. All of nature is functional, and the beauty we intuitively perceive in all natural processes, or by contemplating the imperfect perfection of a flower, is the beauty of *functional design*.

The avatars of child protection, conscious of the fact that morality in its old definition is outmoded, put up a 'new morality' that is sold as functionality and that ultimately has little to do with morality, but much with economics. An alienated child is a better consumer! A child who is early put in daycare profits the economy. And mothers in the work cycle are welcome tax payers.

In addition, child protection favors the dominion of the modern state over the family, the primary breeding cell of the citizen, and the quest of the postmodern state to reign into each and every family.

We have to see that this quest is intrinsically political, and must be understood as political and *not as moral.* Morality in our modern times serves almost everywhere in global culture a pretext function; it is used for manipulating public opinion. Of course, to make their business more effective, the members of the international child protection league have done their best for being backed up by system-conform child care and health professionals, and their publications, so as to let appear the cause of child protection 'a professional necessity.'

This new morality, then, sounds suspiciously similar to the notion of *New World Order* propagated by the Bush administration and comes in a garment that hides its basic irrationality and its fascist, retrograde and paternalistic attitude.

In declaring the child to be an asexual being, the cause of child protection shows that it is basically growth-hostile. In its overall purpose to extend childhood and thus commercial benefits derived from commercializing the child consumer, child protection interferes with children's healthy growth, and especially their emotional and sexual growth.

Child protection fosters not natural growth, but cancerous growth, the growth namely of the infantilization of the child, and even of their parents that the cause of professional child protection declares as 'potentially inadequate' to ensure the total protection of the child. Parents' intuitive and intuitively balanced attitude is generally overruled, if not ridiculed and belittled by the professionals who are signed up with child protection, thereby creating guilt and helplessness in them.

It is easy then to inflict upon both parents and their children the often extremist if not tyrannical measures that enslave the consumer child in a tight corset of state supervision and control. Child protection is potentially the starting hole of a future cause of 'Orwellian' total control, and this danger is so much the more real as apparently nobody or a select few have kept a critical attitude toward this modern form of absolutism and totalitarian control of the citizen.

As the fake arguments of child protection are easy to unveil, simply because in dozens of countries where children are *not* under constant supervision and where they enjoy relative freedom to lovingly copulate with partners outside of the family, child-related crime is a fraction of what it is in Uncle Sam's child protective haven, the purely ideological if not bluntly mercantile root intention of child protection becomes obvious, thereby emasculating its pretended functionality.

Morality has never solved any problems! And child protection is not going to solve the problem of violence against children either, and in the contrary will lead to more child-related crime, and sexual crime!

All research on violence and abuse converges in the insight that abusive relationships are fostered by irresponsibility, infantile attitudes, lack of knowledge, lacking social frameworks for open dialogue and exchange, and by authoritarian forms of control and government.

To put it positively, it has been demonstrated time and again that permissiveness, open exchange, empowerment and consciousness-based forms of education and religion foster nonviolence and peaceful dialogue between all members of society. Hence, for turning down violence and child-related crime, child protection is about the worst and the least effective one could possibly come up with. The truth is that it does not bring a real protection of the child from both violent sex crime in the form of child abduction, child rape and child murder, and domestic violence in the form of forced sexual incest, as the statistics show by themselves.

The *Injury Center of the Centers for Disease Control and Prevention* publishes on their web presence the 2003 statistics for youth violence. In 2003, 5,570 young people ages 10 to 24 were murdered, an average of 15 each day. In 2004, more than 750,000 young people ages 10 to 24 were treated in emergency departments for injuries sustained due to violence.

—http://www.cdc.gov/ViolencePrevention/youthviolence/

(See Statistics Table on the next two pages)

Women who are battered often go to extreme and courageous lengths to protect their children from an abusive partner. In fact, research has shown that the non-abusing parent is often the strongest protective factor in the lives of children who are exposed to domestic violence. However, growing up in a violent home may be a terrifying and traumatic experience that can affect every aspect of a child's life, growth, and development. In spite of this, we know that when properly identified and addressed, the effects of domestic violence on children can be mitigated.

- The U.S. Advisory Board on Child Abuse suggests that domestic violence may be the single major precursor to child abuse and neglect fatalities in this country.[i]

- Studies suggest that between 3.3 and 10 million children are exposed to domestic violence annually.[ii]

- In a national survey of more than 6,000 American families, 50 percent of the men who frequently assaulted their wives also frequently abused their children.[iii]

- Slightly more than half of female victims of intimate violence live in households with children under age 12.[iv]

- Men who as children were exposed to their parents' domestic violence are twice as likely to abuse their own wives than sons of nonviolent parents.[v]

- One study of 2,245 children and teenagers found that recent exposure to violence in the home was a significant factor in predicting a child's violent behavior.[vi]

- Children who are exposed to domestic violence are more likely to exhibit behavioral and physical health problems including depression, anxiety, and violence towards peers.[vii] They are also more likely to attempt suicide, abuse drugs and alcohol, run away from home, engage in teenage prostitution, and commit sexual assault crimes.[viii]

- A recent study of low-income pre-school children in Michigan found that nearly half (46.7 percent) of the children in the study had been exposed to at least one incident of mild or severe violence in the family. Children who had been exposed to violence suffered symptoms of post-traumatic stress disorder, such as bed-wetting or nightmares, and were at greater risk than their peers of having allergies, asthma, gastrointestinal problems, headaches and flu.[ix]

Pregnancy and Domestic Violence

- Each year about 324,000 pregnant women in the U.S. are battered by the men in their lives.[x]

- Complications of pregnancy, including low weight gain, anemia, infections, and first and second trimester bleeding are significantly higher for abused women [xi, xii], as are maternal rates of depression, suicide attempts, tobacco, alcohol, and illicit drug use.[xiii]

[i] U.S. Advisory Board on Child Abuse and Neglect, U.S. Department of Health and Human Services, A Nation's Shame: Fatal Child Abuse and Neglect in the United States: Fifth Report, 1995

[ii] Carlson, Bonnie E. (1984). Children's observations of interpersonal violence. Pp. 147-167 in A.R. Roberts (Ed.) *Battered women and their families* (pp. 147-167). NY: Springer. Straus, M.A. (1992). Children as witnesses to marital violence: A risk factor for lifelong problems among a nationally representative sample of American men and women. *Report of the Twenty-Third Ross Roundtable*. Columbus, OH: Ross Laboratories.

[iii] Strauss, Murray A., Gelles Richard J., and Smith, Christine. 1990. *Physical Violence in American Families; Risk Factors and Adaptations to Violence in 8,145 Families*. New Brunswick: Transaction Publishers.

[iv] U.S. Department of Justice, Violence by Intimates: Analysis of Data on Crimes by Current or Former Spouses, Boyfriends, and Girlfriends, March 1998

[v] Strauss, Murray A., Gelles Richard J., and Smith, Christine. 1990. Physical Violence in American Families; Risk Factors and Adaptations to Violence in 8,145 Families. New Brunswick: Transaction Publishers.

[vi] Singer, M.I., Miller, D.B., Guo, S., Slovak, K & Frieson, T. 1998. "The Mental Health Consequences of Children's Exposure to Violence." Cleveland, OH: Cuyahoga County Community Health Research Institute, Mandel School of Applied Social Sciences, Case Western Reserve University.

[vii] Jaffe, P. and Sudermann, M., "Child Witness of Women Abuse: Research and Community Responses," in Stith, S. and Straus, M., Understanding Partner Violence: Prevalence, Causes, Consequences, and Solutions. Families in Focus Services, Vol. II. Minneapolis, MN: National Council on Family Relations, 1995.

[viii] Wolfe, D.A., Wekerle, C., Reitzel, D. and Gough, R., "Strategies to Address Violence in the Lives of High Risk Youth." In Peled, E., Jaffe, P.G. and Edleson, J.L. (eds.), *Ending the Cycle of Violence: Community Responses to Children of Battered Women*. New York: Sage Publications. 1995.

[ix] Graham-Bermann, Sandra A and Julie Seng. 2005. "Violence Exposure and Traumatic Stress Symptoms as Additional Predictors of Health Problems in High-Risk Children." *Journal of Pediatrics*. 146(3):309-10.

[x] Gazmararian JA, Petersen R, Spitz AM, Goodwin MM, Saltzman LE, Marks JS. 2000. "Violence and Reproductive Health: Current Knowledge and Future Research Directions." *Maternal and Child Health Journal*. 4(2):79-84.

[xi] Parker, B., McFarlane, J., & Soeken, K. 1994. "Abuse During Pregnancy: Effects on Maternal Complications and Infant Birthweight in Adult and Teen Women." *Obstetrics & Gynecology*. 841: 323-328.

[xii] McFarlane, J. Parker B., & Soeken, K. 1996. "Abuse during Pregnancy: Association with Maternal Health and Infant Birthweight." *Nursing Research*. 45:32-37.

[xiii] McFarlane, J., Parker, B., & Soeken, K. 1996. "Physical Abuse, Smoking and Substance Abuse During Pregnancy: Prevalence, Interrelationships and Effects on Birthweight." *Journal of Obstetrical Gynecological and Neonatal Nursing*. 25: 313-320.

—Source: Family Violence Prevention Fund. (Id.)

CHAPTER SEVEN

The Importance of Sensuality

One of the greatest pitfalls in the media debate about 'normalizing pedophilia' is the more or less *deliberate confusion* between shared sensual love as part of a friendship bond between an adult and a child, on one hand, and sexual violence in the form of a genital assault on a child by either a stranger or a family friend, on the other. The two entirely different situational, sexual and cognitive experiences are thrown in one meltpot of irrational and most of the time polemic debate that is manipulatory rather than informational in that it intends to backbone the state-funded enslavement of the consumer child!

Such an attitude and polemics is truly criminal; that today a majority of professionals and policy makers are involved in this propaganda does not alter this fact. It is a signal for the *depravation and decadence* of Western society to have arrived at this point of confusion and betrayal of true love. The current trend toward a new era of fascism is one direct result of this life denial; while the trend is especially visible in the United States and France, it is something that has affected all Western nations, and the majority of all nations on earth today, who stupidly follow the madness and millenary perversion of patriarchy as a movement against nature.

This trend favors and purports information filtering, the denial of complexity, and the resurgence of intolerance and rampant irrationality, political hegemony and international neocolonialism, together with the rampant turndown of democratic values that started with the 1990s; it is characterized by an obsessional public focus on so-called 'perverse sexuality'.

This is not as surprising as it seems on first sight; in fact, it can be shown historically that in periods of fundamentalism, political tyranny and religious oppression, all natural expressions like emotions and sexuality are feared and demonized, while at the same time truly perverse forms of sexuality, that is coercive and violent sex, as well as sexual torture, are secretly practiced by juntas, militia and extremists of all kinds. As a general rule, all what is loudly and polemically attacked and rejected as 'abject and perverse' in any given society is what is secretly practiced and what that society is at pains with! It's the shadow that invariably comes about through denial.

And there is *more shadow* even when there is an abundance of light, as it is typically in societies that adhere to what Joseph Campbell termed the *solar worldview*. All, in these societies, officially is light and sunshine as it were, and there is a strong emphasis on 'doing good', so-called 'values,' and political leadership tends to be joyfully conservative, simple-minded, dogmatic, and brutal-righteous in an almost archaic sense.

What by far dominates the scene in the daily media is how tough and mighty police, security and military forces are, how well they protect the populace and how brilliantly they operate. That these are but paper values, and that behind the sunny boy faces of those politicians and the sunshine smile of the all-present big brother, there is rampant misery both socially and in relationships, social injustice, brutality, power abuse and insecurity, only a select few grasp it, and dare to acknowledge it in public.

In such a climate, real dialogue and exchange is as good as impossible, especially when complex issues are debated that cannot be tackled by applying mechanistic and simplistic strategies and methods.

Violence is exactly such a highly complex and difficult-to-grasp topic, and it has penetrated psychology only quite recently, In fact, one of the major insights this research brought about was that without understanding the flowing, electric and ethereal nature of human emotions and the importance of sensuality and sane irrationality, violence cannot be creatively understood.

Violence truly is the antithesis to sensuality.

A human being can be violent *only after a more or less prolonged period of sensual starving* that usually begins in early childhood or even as early as in infancy. Violence has no roots in the human setup. It is a *conditioned response*, not a natural one.

Wilhelm Reich's early sex research found in addition that even basically nonviolent people's sexual response gets more violent after a prolonged period of sexual starving, which typically also means *sensual starving* because of the lack of tactile contact!

This manifests often in an outbreak of what later is qualified as *domestic violence* but was in fact a foreplay for the sexual mating between the partners, only that the male who was sensually starved, needed to beat his partner before touching her sexually!

Beating has been seen as frequent by Reich in all of his patients who went through periods of sensual starving, both in sex fantasies and as a stimulant during actual mating. What is interesting about these findings is that they were not only assessed with generally violent persons nor with persons who experienced sensual deprivation during their childhood, but *with people who were psychiatrically assessed as being normal and adequate.* What can also be observed in this context is that the beating will occur as an accompanying behavior only during the first mating after the prolonged sensual starvation, and not subsequently with the same partner.

This is an additional signal for the fact that the violent response was triggered through the starvation and is not, as could be wrongly assumed, a generally sadistic form of sexual response with these persons!

Sexual sadism as a relative perversion of the sexual response can be affirmed only in case the person *cannot reach a sexual orgasm without the additional violent behavior during the sexual mating.* Here the violence inflicted on the partner is a *condition* for the person being orgasmic in the sexual game.

The same is valid, vice versa, for the masochistic person, who needs to experience sexual encounters spiced in specific ways through violent behavior suffered. Here too, the overall orgasmic response is conditioned upon the reception of these specific forms of violence – not any kind of violence.

I must probably make it clear that I do not talk about *Sadomasochism (SM)* when I am talking about sexual violence. I do not find it problematic when two adults agree to have violent sex, on either side of the game table, so to speak. This can be a problem for moralists only but sociopolitically, and as a matter of policy making, sadomasochism is not a problem, neither ethically nor for society as a whole. It's however an interesting research topic because we are not born as sadists and masochists, and the research why persons are sensitive and receptive for certain forms of sexual violence, or for violence that is in itself non-sexual but that accompanies the mating game, can be highly revealing; it will show in every individual case story why the person has been conditioned to the specific forms of violence that trigger in them the orgasmic response.

This is so because the violent behavior *has become sexualized.* Most often, physical and humiliating, and somehow also sexually tinted physical punishment inflicted by parents or a tutelary adult was the trigger. Thus most of these case stories show that the affliction has its roots in childhood and adolescence.

CHAPTER EIGHT

Social Policy Considerations

What imports me to convey in this context is the much more general problem of sensual love being seen on the same line of reasoning in policy making as sexual violence. One must be really schizoid to not make a distinction here, but it seems that in our Western nations today the majority is indeed to that point schizophrenic because the confusion between sensual love and sexual violence is so pronounced in the media, the anti-pornography debate, the child pornography and child abuse debate and the completely distorted debate, if there is any at all, about 'missing children'. Hence, there is really a need to put the finger on the wound and separate apples from pears!

When an adult and a child caress each other because there is love, erotic attraction, care and sensual excitation on both sides, no line can be drawn that says:

- until such and such point, the behavior is to be considered as the normal and sensual care-giving of a caretaker for a child;

- from such and such point, the behavior of the adult is to be considered as child abuse because (s)he got sexually aroused and in addition touched certain private parts of the child.

Let me start with the analysis of a *borderline* case because it is especially these cases that show the perversity and madness the public discussion of these matters is pervaded with. Once the public has lost its reasoning mind, we can't expect it to reason more sanely, then, in cases that seem to be clear-cut, when it's namely question of full sexual penetration and aggravated cases where the copulation was forced, or even where the child was murdered either during or after the intercourse.

What I am saying is that the mainstream way of reasoning shows with much evidence that *no real difference is made between sensual love and sexual violence* because the difference is simply not understood, or it is well understood but not socially and legally *cognized and recognized!*

I will show further down that in the United States most sex laws do not make a big difference in punishing a true lover of a child, who had a sensual, loving and consenting relation with the child and where no penetration was attempted, and somebody who violently assaulted a child sexually, penetrated the child and inflicted great harm on the child.

The punishment for both types of offenders is approximately twenty years of prison, and experience with the situation of law enforcement in Britain and the United States has shown the striking perversity that the *nonviolent and caregiving childlover will in prison be exposed to much greater violence, and also sexual violence*, from the side of inmates than the violent sex offender who assaulted a child, if he did not outright murder the child.

—See, for example, A.J. Davis, Sexual Assaults in the Philadelphia Prison System and Sherriff's Van (1968), A.M. Scarro Jr. (ed.), Male Rape (1982). See also Interview with Brett Portman in P. A. N. 15, 29-39 (1983) and Edward Brongersma, Aggression against Pedophiles, 7 International Journal of Law & Psychiatry 82 (1984), with further references. More spectacular even is the decision of the Supreme Court of Sweden who, in 1980, refused to extradite to the USA a Kentucky physician who got a prison sentence of 59 years for harmless play with boys. The long sentence and the inhuman conditions in American prisons were given as reasons for the refusal to extradite. According to Alvin Bronstein, Director of the NPP for the American Civil Liberties Union, this was the first time that a foreign nation has refused to extradite a person to the US in a non-political case because of American prison conditions (PAN 4, 6 (1980), citing The Hapotoc Collective, Amsterdam, NL, as reporting source).

In addition, it is established in forensic psychiatry that the nonviolent pedophile and the child-assaulting and child-murdering offender are *two entirely different personalities*, and that their forensic history and etiology is equally different. Child rapists and murderers are most often *not pedophiles* and do not label themselves as such; they also show in their sexual history typically a pattern of more or less violent heterosexuality with singular or repeated incidence of rape, before they began to assault children sexually. Or they have been sexual virgins prior to assaulting a child sexually, and in these cases the incidence of murder is especially high!

Many of those, on the other hand, who are in for nonviolent erotic relations with children are *teachers, nurses or doctors* and have had no criminal record prior to the incidence. Many of them are academics, with sometimes a high level of academic achievement. Another social group frequently involved with these kind of trials nowadays are priests. The sexual details of these cases are quite uniform in that there is hardly an incidence of penetration, but generally fondling, caressing, kissing, licking, and masturbation, often accompanied by photographing the nude child or both partners during their loving embrace.

At a time when it was unknown how important sensuality is in nutritive child-rearing, it is no wonder that sex laws were drafted that punished people for being naturally sensual with a child, or for giving a child tactile stimulation in the form of caresses, kisses, tender fondling and by licking the child's skin. But this fundamentally changed since the 1960s and 70s, when neurology, anthropology and skin research coincided in showing that one of the surest factors in the etiology of violence is emotional and tactile deprivation of infants, children and adolescents through insufficient or inadequate nursing.

By the time of finalizing this book, in 2010, it is established doctrine in psychology, education and the mental health professions that tactile stimulation and emotionally abundant and empathetic parenting is *one of the ways to reduce violence both domestically and structurally.* These strategies are now also supported and encouraged by most Western governments.

It has been demonstrated that modern attitudes such as mechanistic and hospital-based childbirth and many modern child-rearing practices were not conducive to the healthy growth of children, and solutions were found in old traditions, and through the reintegration of methods practiced at the time of our grandparents.

Obstetrics and a large part of pediatrics were revolutionized through these new insights or because knowledge our grandparents already had was eventually acknowledged by official pediatrics; as a result, many of the truly harmful practices were disfavored and abandoned, such as the nonsensical separation of mother and infant subsequent to birth, or the obsessive habit to put children to bed at well-defined sleeping hours instead of letting them go to bed when they are naturally tired.

Thus, today we can say that we know as a society how important it is to *touch* children, to give them abundant emotional and sensual nutrition, and to raise them in a climate of tolerance and acceptance that is widely free of taboos. We also know today that most children who suicide themselves do so because of emotional, tactile, sensual and/or sexual starvation suffered in a milieu that does not foster dialogue, that is fundamentalist, moralistic and cold.

It has been found with quite a surprise that, on the other hand, children who suffer even long-term abuse but are touched, while not touched in a friendly and respectful manner, but are touched anyway, that is in the form of beating and caning, are less likely to run away from home or commit suicide. It has been found invariably and repeatedly that the most harmful form of child abuse simply is *ignorance* and *child neglect* as a result of a sheer disinterest in the child.

When we apply this knowledge to our initial question or definition of the problem of distinguishing sensual love from sexual assault, we see that sensual love can only be qualified as *harmless* in the sense of non-harmful to the child, and that it is even conducive to foster abundant emotional and tactile care for the child!

On the other hand, in violent sexual assault of a child, all these care-giving qualities are absent, and obviously so, because the intention of the offender is not caring for another, but aggressing another for whatever purpose, be it easy sexual satisfaction, be it a sadistic acting-out of violence suffered as an act of projective retaliation, be it as a compensation for abuse suffered early in childhood, be it as an act of retaliation against society as a whole by victimizing a beautiful little girl or boy, because the child is considered as the most cherished symbol of beauty and happiness in modern democratic society.

It has been found through forensic research that the brutal child kidnapper, rapist and killer not seldom has a *hidden agenda* against the whole of society and that the criminal act is intended 'as a matter of revenge', where retaliation is put on stage in a drama enacted with the deliberate intent to inflict harm not only on the child victim himself or herself, but on a whole range of potentially affected people, if not society as a whole.

In such cases, to repeat it, the abduction and rape of the child, and often also subsequent murder of the victim are steps in a process of *emotional abreaction* where the offender seeks a compensatory satisfaction for hurt suffered earlier in their own life. That this satisfaction is an illusion and that in the contrary the hurt will be greatly aggravated through the hurt done to not only the child but to many other suffering agents, such as the child's parents and teachers, social workers, nurses, doctors, police agents and all those involved in such dramatic cases, these offenders usually do not see and can probably not see because of their specific affliction and the distortion of their perception, which is part of their sexual and nonsexual sadism pattern.

Sadism leads to a gradual but fatal *desensibilization* and *desensitization* on all levels of the personality, and it also negatively affects cognitive abilities. This does not mean that these offenders are mentally ill or have to be exempted from law enforcement because of mental disturbance that affected their insight in right or wrong; but it means that they have developed a level of general brutality prior to the offense that has its roots in extended periods of emotional, tactile, sensual and often also sexual starvation suffered earlier in their lives.

CHAPTER NINE

Quest for a Distinction

These explanations that I forward here based upon my knowledge and experience as a lawyer, forensic researcher and consultant, suffice to illustrate my point that violent sexual assault on children cannot be put in one pot with sensual and nonviolent love with a child only because in the latter relationship some or the other erotically tinted exchange has taken place, if this exchange is to be legally defined as 'sexual' or not.

Sexuality does not alter its generally healthy and growth-fostering character when it's an exchange between loving and consenting people, only because on one side of the game table is a child. To see this requires one to be free of sexual anxiety; to have had traumatic sexual experiences, early or later in life, and feeling 'as a victim' as a result is not an excuse for damaging children through child-rearing attitudes that are based upon tactile, sensual and sexual deprivation.

To put it in simpler terms: sex is healthy food for all members of society, not just for grown-ups, if our laws accept this truth in the present moment or not is not the question. I will show further down that our sex laws are the successors of canon law, the body of law erected by the Church, and that they as such have no rational basis.

Once the difference between sensual love and violent sexual assault has been cognized, it will be evident that nonviolent, sensual and consenting encounters between adults and children where sexual caresses have been exchanged, cannot be reasonably subjected, within a democratic society, to criminal law, but have to be considered not only by informed experts, but by the legislator as adequate and *socially acceptable social conduct.*

The quintessence of all research on the relationship between pleasure and violence is the thesis that cultures that continue to be highly repressive regarding the emotional and tactile needs of small children and that, in addition, prohibit premarital sex, will end in a chaos of violence and destruction that has not seen an equal in human history!

Violence, as Dr. James W. Prescott states authoritatively, and with an abundant amount of evidence, is a compensation reaction of the human brain for the deprivation of tactile pleasure. Prescott identifies our present confusion between sex and sensuality in the Biblical and Jewish traditions that are the foundation of American or, more generally, Western society. The logical conclusions of this interconnectedness are:

- the more a person has received tactile nutrition during her early years, the more she has known body pleasure from childhood, the more her pleasure areas will be activated and, as a result, the more her violence areas will be inhibited; as a result, such a person will be generally peaceful and peace-loving;

- the more a person was deprived of tactile pleasure during childhood, the more her desire for body pleasure was repressed or body pleasure experienced as a guilt-producing activity, the more the person's pleasure areas will be inhibited and, as a result, the more her violence areas will be active; as a result, such a person will be generally violent and will tend to justify social, structural, educational violence or violence as part of law enforcement.

Interestingly, this research gave rise to the insight that tactile deprivation in early childhood does not automatically lead to a violent character. There are namely factors that compensate for early tactile deprivation, the most decisive of those factors being *premarital sex*. In this point resides the specific appeal for a peace-oriented future national and international policy on fighting violence. Such policies must include, according to Prescott, the recognition of children's rights, by law, for a reasonably unregulated emotional and sexual life.

I would add here that this right also encompasses *free choice relations for children* and the freedom or the child to build and pursue friendships with peers and adults that are based upon mutual erotic attraction.

The recognition of *tactile sexuality,* which is sexuality without penetration, today stands out as the antithesis to the act-based sexual approach of the Church's law givers and Cartesian mechanistic sexology that we are presently transcending. Today even conservatives begin to consider a traditional act-centered view of sexuality as outmoded; however, the ethical consequences of this profound paradigm change are often not seen or are not acknowledged. The present public discussion about sex is rigid and impregnated with various fears and taboos. The mythic image of the 'sexual perpetrator' if not *sexual terminator* is haunting present-day American talk shows and general information about sexuality often portrays sexual behavior in a rush with misunderstood Darwinism as *innately predatory*, especially with the male.

> —For the myths of predator sexuality, and pedophile predator sexuality, see in particular Peter Fritz Walter, Pedophilia Revisited: The Making of a Crime for Justifying Lacking Social Policy (Essays on Law, Policy and Psychiatry, Vol. 8, 2018).

The general hysteria about abusive or non-abusive sex with children is all-pervasive in the American media culture. This general attitude is far from being supportive for the tactile needs of present-day Western children! The obsessive focus on protecting children can easily be revealed as either a lip service, or a new money-making device, or else another way to enslave children within a doctrinaire consumer ideology that is based on no other values than huge worldwide financial success for the multinationals that directly or indirectly profit from the sexless child.

CHAPTER TEN

Morality has always been held to play an important role in the education of children, in our patriarchal tradition and history. And it is morality that is generally advanced to justify educational violence.

I will take reference in the present chapter to the astounding *Declaration of the United Nations' General Assembly from 29 August 2006* that bears the signature of Paulo Sérgio Pinheiro, Secretary-General of the United Nations. The declaration is an important additional backup research for the *International Convention on the Rights of the Child*, UNICEF, 1989.

—The Convention entered into force September 2, 1990. It is officially published here: http://www.unicef.org/crc/

In the brilliantly researched paper at the basis of the declaration, there are a number of painful facts that are worth mentioning in some length because the mass media in most countries try to hide them as good as they can.

One reason for what Alice Miller called *society's betrayal of the child* is that any public criticism on how children are mistreated 'in the name of their own best' *would inevitably reflect back on the mainstream paradigm of lawful educational violence.*

—See Alice Miller, Thou Shalt Not Be Aware (1998).

This is so because the only rationale for cruelty inflicted upon children in the name of the child's welfare is *morality*.

From a rational perspective, there is no reason why violence, which has after long research found to be damaging for all members of society, should exceptionally be harmless and beneficial when inflicted upon children as its weakest members.

What angers me is that organizations like the United Nations, or national governmental departments never mention the fact that all cruelty inflicted upon children as educational measures are imbedded in the age-old belief that children had to be bettered through *morality*. The very idea of finding nature inadequate and faulty, and the hubris to thus 'better nature' through the intellectual, emotional, cognitive and sexual manipulation of children is a religious perversion, and it was practiced, as I already mentioned, by *Calvinism*, a form of religious fanaticism that indulged in unmatched brutality against children.

> —Alice Miller's books, especially the one quoted in the previous note, contain horrifying examples of educational cruelty inflicted upon children in the name of their own best; the most perverse tortures of children were inflicted by Calvinism.

Another author who has brilliantly analyzed the educational brutality against children under patriarchy, and its psychological reasons, is Riane Eisler, already mentioned. In her book *The Chalice and the Blade (1995)*, she retraces the process of what she calls the 'truncation of civilization,' the rise of patriarchy in all its forms, and its present-day dominance in Western society, but also the signals for its current and future transformation.

While Riane Eisler is outspoken and explicit, in her second book *Sacred Pleasure (1996)*, with regard to our individual and collective need for eroticism and a culture that integrates the beauty and strength of natural sexuality, she never with one word mentions *children's right for sexual freedom* in the sense not just of auto-eroticism, but as the right to build and pursue erotic friendships with peers and adults outside of the family!

The reasons for this silence are obvious to me; in a climate of bewilderment, confusion and persecution that is one result of many in what I came to call the 'abuse-centered culture', a really open and public debate about the question of children's sexual life has been rendered impossible by the prevailing sociopolitical forces.

I know from my own twelve years of publishing experience that any author who even slightly advocates a liberalization of children's freedom and erotic autonomy suffers the inevitable fate of being rejected in mainstream publishing and otherwise is relegated to self-publishing.

Besides that, authors who tread this daring path, including myself, are academically discredited, if they are not simply labeled as child abusers. And yet, I find it outright coward from the side of most professional authors to shut up in the face of the obvious bias of the current media debate on child abuse and child sexuality, while knowing better than the mass public and their polemic press and slaughter-politicians.

The persistent coward muteness of those who have the authority to shift the trend in another direction is a *sign of moral and social corruption* after all, and a signal that we are not far from gliding into another abyss of fascist control and tyranny in a near future.

In addition, international organizations have since long practiced a politics of extreme conservatism in this respect, and their publications generally do all but criticize morality as the ultimate culprit behind the plague of violence.

CHAPTER
ELEVEN

The Turndown of International Adoption

I remember having had several talks in the UNICEF headquarters in Geneva, back in 1984, about the starting turndown of international adoption. The director in that office and active purporter of that policy was a woman who said to have been abused early in her life; she saw in adoption only that: *abuse*. For her, an emotionally frigid character very similar to Amanda in the film *What the Bleep Do We Know*, abuse was the rule and adoption was but an open door toward rampant abuse. Hence, adoption had to be turned down! I have seen the follow-up of this policy in the upcoming years.

In 1986, I met a family in Switzerland who had adopted an infant in Bogotá, Colombia. The Swiss government allowed them to take the baby on an interim status, while the final decision was said to take one to two years. After one year, the decision was made and the adoption was declined—with the result that the family had to render the baby back into poverty and despair in Colombia. The reason was purely administrative as the couple went through all psychological tests fully approved and also had the financial means to support the child.

And I remembered that administrative figure I had met in UNICEF headquarters just two years prior to this incident and her bursting out in: 'Pedophiles have to be stopped buying babies in Bogotá!'

In 1997, Vietnam changed their government policy on adoption, applying under the pressure of UNICEF much stricter rules for adoption, which in most cases turns out for the applicant to being obliged to make actually *two full adoptions*, the first one in their home country, the second one in Vietnam. The previous procedure, which had been a question of months, was then becoming a matter of *one or two years and endless administrative hurdles.*

In 2004, I have seen adoption turned down completely in Cambodia for both the United States and France. Upon my inquiry with the *Ministry of Education and Social Affairs* in Phnom Penh, I was informed that in the case of France, Cambodia had turned down adoption for reasons not given, and in the case of the United States, adoption was said to have been turned down by the American government.

In the months to follow, I have seen an American woman arrested, who was famed worldwide for her facilitating adoption in Cambodia. She was lodged in the exclusive *Raffles 'Le Royal' Hotel* in Phnom Penh and operated from her office suite in that hotel for almost twenty years. She had facilitated adoption from Cambodia for thousands of American parents.

The information I received from her showed that she was particularly severe in screening applicants, more even than most governments, that the medical and mental health precautions were particularly tight with her procedure, and that also a quite considerable financial hurdle was built in the whole procedure: the price was around eleven thousand dollars for adopting one single child. The headquarters of her organization had been in the United States.

Her sudden arrest was a shock for the intelligentsia in Phnom Penh, so much the more as the true reasons for the arrest never having penetrated the media. This rendered the incident even more mysterious. All had the appearance of a scapegoat affair that was put on stage as a signal for a *political policy change on highest level.*

When you consider that this woman had been operating even before the Pol Pot era and had been evacuated back to the States during the political tyranny, for coming back to Cambodia after the war and operated all through the years, in full public presence, with all papers in order, and in cooperating on a daily basis with both Cambodian and American governmental authorities, the story really sounds unbelievable!

In 2006, India changed their policy on adoption, a trend that began first in the Christian-dominated (!) province of Kerala and from there was promoted nationwide. The measure was explained to me in an interview with by the Head of Social Affairs of Kerala in Trivandrum, in December 2006, with the words: 'India will foster adoption henceforth only for its own nationals, not for foreigners anymore.'

A further reason was not given, except the remark that the change of the government policy on adoption had been taken on highest level and was 'in accordance with international regulations, especially those promoted by UNICEF and the United Nations.' That explained it all.

In June 2007, China radically changed their policy on adoption. It was argued that adoption as practiced in China had been criticized since long by Western-driven NGOs and especially UNICEF. It had been considered as 'too liberal,' which is why the Chinese government had restricted it. The controls and screening of applicants had been raised to a level unprecedented in Chinese history.

One example penetrated into the media just prior to the enactment of the new policy, in May 2007, the case of an American social worker in her forties, whose body weight was one hundred fifty kilograms.

The Chinese government bluntly declared such an applicant as *unfit for adoption* and wrote to her in the refusal of adoption something like 'as she was not even able to cope with her obesity, how would she think she could cope with the difficulties of raising an adoptive child from China?' The decision was felt like an insult and the American government tried to conciliate because the affair had been mediatized a lot, and not for the best of everybody involved.

This is exactly what the former adoption policy that has been abandoned now by most governments tried to avoid: the more or less arbitrary reject of an applicant for reasons either faked, or never told, or because not pleasing enough to the decision-makers on adoption!

The new policy that was coined and promoted since the beginning of the 1980s by UNICEF opens the door to all kinds of abuse and thought control from the side of governments for rejecting an applicant. This is how UNICEF and most other international organizations and NGOs are working for the best of the child! I spare any further comment and will instead get into details of the before-mentioned declaration on the rights of the child, and the extensive research that it contains and references.

As a general remark, from the side of an international lawyer, I join those who openly declared that after the unprecedented invasion of Iraq by the United States against the Veto of the United Nations, the UN has lost its mandate and has no more significance in easing and regulating international relations and in facilitating world peace. I know that the same is true for UNICEF, and *especially* for UNICEF.

The United States do since years not pay their contribution to this organization they are a member of, for the reason of criticizing some bad budgetary operations of UNICEF. Needless to add that this is not allowed by the UN Charter and is violating international law.

Back in 1985, I met a French ambassador in Switzerland who said to have founded a number of orphanages in Khartoum, Sudan. He said the French government never gave a single penny for this humanitarian endeavor and that all the money received was from private donators. He explained that all his efforts were constantly meeting with opposition from the side of UNICEF and that they had absolutely no intention for improving the desperate situation of orphans in Sudan, who are full orphans, with no parent or relative left, because of rampant genocide practiced in some regions in Sudan.

This is typically presented in a distorted manner in the mass media anywhere in the world. I had my reasons to never join an international organization while I am fully qualified for such a position as an international lawyer and doctor of law with a specialization on public international law. That is also the reason that I do not honestly believe that the declaration on children's rights or any other child-related policy making from the side of old-fashioned international organizations will bring any real change in the world. All these organizations were established by Colonial powers and were never really accepted by the majority of countries, which namely formerly were subjected to the Colonial regime of exactly the powers that founded the new organizations in order to 'protect the losers from losing more.'

There is no morality in international politics and the social traffic of nations! Decisions are made for obvious reasons that regard the vital interests of the nation states themselves, and not for any other reasons. If children are concerned or soldiers, weapons or drugs, it makes no difference. Morality is a fictitious and highly effective tool for controlling the mass mind, but it has nothing ever to do with goodness, good actions, or anything related to decency or harmonious human affairs.

The reason why *moralistic arguments* are used as the number one rhetoric tool in all humanitarian debates, especially those that regard children, is that it's the easiest way to lie, and to betray the public about the true motivations of national and international policy making.

Chapter Twelve

Child Play vs. Morality

After this foreplay, I shall now discuss some revealing details from the research done at the basis of the *Declaration on the Rights of the Child* that was adopted by the UN's General Assembly in August 2006.

In fact, already the very first sentence voiced in the declaration emphasizes the universality of the problem of violence against children, and there are no exceptions made for countries like the United States, who notoriously are about to see the problem with others, diligently denying it for their own nation.

No violence against children is justifiable; all violence against children is preventable. Yet the in-depth study on violence against children (the

Study) confirms that such violence exists in every country of the world, cutting across culture, class, education, income and ethnic origin. In every region, in contradiction to human rights obligations and children's developmental needs, violence against children is socially approved, and is frequently legal and State-authorized.

—UN-Doc. A/61/299 of August 29, 2006, A, I, 1, p. 5.

What is unique in this study, and different from the current child sexuality policy, children themselves were heard by the expert group and could voice their suggestions for better protection from violence (A, I, 4).

It is also significant that the experts were not lured in the old morality debate that justifies violence against children with the typical arguments forwarded by paternalistic society: tradition and discipline. (A, I, 2).

Eventually, the expert group also emphasizes what I pointed out in this study and other books of mine, that is, violence 'is multidimensional and calls for a multifaceted response' (A, I, 5).

A particularly important sector of violence against children is *education* and the so-called *reeducation of delinquent children and adolescents.* Here, the report is particularly honest and revealing and truly has merit. As an introduction to this complex of questions, the report states:

> Societal acceptance of violence is also an important factor: both children and perpetrators may accept physical, sexual and psychological violence as inevitable and normal. Discipline through physical and humiliating punishment, bullying and sexual harassment are frequently perceived as normal, particularly when no visible or lasting physical injury results. The lack of an explicit legal prohibition of corporal punishment reflects this. According to the Global Initiative to End All Corporal Punishment of Children, at least 106 countries do not prohibit the use of corporal punishment in schools, 147 countries do not prohibit it within alternative care settings, and as yet only 16 countries have prohibited its use in the home.

—UN-Doc. A/61/299 of August 29, 2006, I, A, 26, p. 9.

The report summarizes the emerging picture in part II, B, 28, in six points:

> ▸ WHO has estimated, through the use of limited country-level data, that almost 53,000 children died worldwide in 2002 as a result of homicide.

- Studies from many countries in all regions of the world suggest that up to 80 to 98 per cent of children suffer physical punishment in their homes, with a third or more experiencing severe physical punishment resulting from the use of implements.

- Reporting on a wide range of developing countries, the Global School-based Health Survey recently found that between 20 and 65 per cent of school-aged children reported having been verbally or physically bullied in the past 30 days. Bullying is also frequent in industrialized countries.

- WHO estimates that 150 million girls and 73 million boys under 18 experienced forced sexual intercourse or other forms of sexual violence during 2002.

- According to a WHO estimate, between 100 and 140 million girls and women in the world have undergone some form of female genital mutilation/cutting. Estimates from UNICEF published in 2005 suggest that in sub-Saharan Africa, Egypt and the Sudan, 3 million girls and women are subjected to genital mutilation/cutting every year.

- Recent ILO estimates indicate that, in 2004, 218 million children were involved in child labour, of whom 126 million were in hazardous work. Estimates from 2000 suggest that 5.7 million were in forced or bonded labour, 1.8 million in prostitution and pornography, and 1.2 million were victims of trafficking. However, compared with estimates published in 2002, the incidence of child labour has diminished by 11 per cent and 25 per cent fewer children were found working in hazardous occupations. (Id., pp. 9-10, with further references).

What is interesting in the report is that sexual violence is cited here in the explicit formulation as *forced sexual intercourse* and other forms of sexual violence. No allusion was made as to sexual mating between children and adults that took place in a setting where the child consented, even though that consent may not be deemed valid by the laws of the place, but where the child explicitly or implicitly expressed a *willingness* for sexual interaction with the adult.

If the report left that open to further study or if it does not consider it, in accordance with my own distinction, as sexual violence, is open to further discussion. But as an intermediary conclusion it is certainly important to note that the study *did not expressly subsume nonviolent and consenting erotic encounters between adults and children as sexual violence inflicted upon a child.*

And here it stands out against what the most fanatic avatars in the international league of child protection today purport and practice, in that for them it all boils down to the same because they consider sex to be the damaging factor, and not violence.

In the contrary, the study clearly emphasizes the devastating effects of violence, and also of physical, educational violence that hitherto most government reports try to belittle or play down. The report states:

> - 41. Violence against children in the family may frequently take place in the context of discipline and takes the form of physical, cruel or humiliating punishment. Harsh treatment and punishment in the family are common in both industrialized and developing countries. Children, as reported in studies and speaking for themselves during the study's regional consultations, highlighted the physical and psychological hurt they suffer as a result of these forms of treatment and proposed positive and effective alternative forms of discipline.

> - 42. Physical violence is often accompanied by psychological violence. Insults, name-calling, isolation, rejection, threats, emotional indifference and belittling are all forms of violence that can be detrimental to a child's psychological development and well-being –

especially when it comes from a respected adult such as a parent. It is of critical importance that parents be encouraged to employ exclusively non- violent methods of discipline. (Id., III, B, 41-42, p. 13, with further references).

Further down, the report focuses on the *aggravating circumstance* that the child is female, as more violence has been seen to occur against female children compared to violence suffered by male children.

What is important to note here is that the report emphasizes as a potential risk in child marriage the danger for the girl to suffer *coercive sex*, not just marital sex in the ordinary understanding of the word. Second, it is interesting that *some Western countries are mentioned in the report regarding traditional practices of female genital mutilation* that in the mass media of those countries, and here especially the United States, are almost always attributed to African or Arabic populations, and often in an implicitly defamatory way attributed to Islam or Islamic minorities such as the Taliban:

> ▸ 45. Absence of legally established minimum ages for sexual consent and marriage in some countries may expose children to partner

violence. Eighty-two million girls are estimated to marry before age 18. A significant number are married at much younger ages, frequently coercively, and face a high risk of violence, including forced sex.

> ▸ 46. Harmful traditional practices affect children disproportionately and are generally imposed on them at an early age by their parents or community leaders. According to the Special Rapporteur on traditional practices affecting the health of women and the girl child, female genital mutilation, which, according to WHO, is carried out on increasingly younger girls, is prevalent in Africa, and also occurs in some parts of Asia and within immigrant communities in Europe, Australia, Canada and the United States of America. Other harmful traditional practices affecting children include *binding, scarring, burning, branding, violent initiation rites, fattening, forced marriage, so-called honour crimes and dowry-related violence, exorcism, or witchcraft. (Id., III, A, 45-46, p. 14, with further references).*

The perhaps most important part of the report is C. 'Violence in care and justice systems'. Before quoting the most relevant passages from the report below, let me emphasize as an international lawyer that until today, *no human rights protection has been enforced for juvenile offenders and delinquents* for protecting them against abuses suffered in correctional institutions, *while for adult offenders such protection is assured in most countries*, and for ordinary and partly also for political prisoners. This is by itself a revolting fact that to my knowledge many people simply ignore, or not even bother about, while they may on the other hand be on the side of the most fanatic child protectors when it concerns the slightest experience of a child with sex. There is about no topic of public discussion that is to that point distorted and actually borders ridicule! It simply cannot be taken serious, and solutions, socially and legally, should therefore be worked out by experts, without asking the moron populace about their anyway completely manipulated opinions.

> ▸ 53. Millions of children, particularly boys, spend substantial periods of their lives under the control and supervision of care authorities or justice systems, and in institutions such as orphanages, children's homes, care homes, police lock-ups, prisons, juvenile detention facilities and reform schools. These children are at risk of violence from staff and officials responsible for their well-being. Corporal punishment in institutions is not explicitly prohibited in a majority of countries.

> ▸ 54. Overcrowding and squalid conditions, societal stigmatization and discrimination, and poorly trained staff heighten the risk of violence.

Effective complaints, monitoring and inspection mechanisms, and adequate government regulation and oversight are frequently absent. *Not all perpetrators are held accountable, creating a culture of impunity and tolerance of violence against children.* The impact of institutionalization goes beyond the experience by children of violence. Long-term effects can include severe developmental delays, disability, irreversible psychological damage, and increased rates of suicide and recidivism.

▸ 55. As many as 8 million of the world's children are in residential care. Relatively few are in such care because they have no parents, but most are in care because of disability, family disintegration, violence in the home, and social and economic conditions, including poverty.

▸ 56. Violence by institutional staff, for the purpose of disciplining children, includes *beatings with hands, sticks and hoses, and hitting children's heads against the wall, restraining children in cloth sacks, tethering them to furniture, locking them in freezing rooms for days at a time and leaving them to lie in their own excrement. (Id., III, C, 53-56, p. 16, with further references)*

▸ 61. Despite the obligation to ensure that the detention of children shall be used only as a measure of last resort and for the shortest appropriate period of time contained in article 37 of the Convention on the Rights of the Child, it was estimated in 1999 that 1 million children are deprived of their liberty. Most of these are charged with minor or petty crimes, and are first-time offenders. Many are detained because of truancy, vagrancy or homelessness. In some countries, the majority of children in detention have not been convicted of a crime, but are awaiting trial.

▸ 62. Children in detention are frequently subjected to violence by staff, including as a form of control or punishment, often for minor infractions. In at least 77 countries corporal and other violent punishments are accepted as legal disciplinary measures in penal institutions. Children may be beaten, caned, painfully restrained, and subjected to humiliating treatment such as being stripped naked and caned in front of other detainees. Girls in detention facilities are at particular risk of physical and sexual abuse, mainly when supervised by male staff. (Id., III, C, 61-62, p. 14, with further references)

The details of this report on children subjected to all kinds of torture once they are labeled by society as 'juvenile offenders' may be shocking for many people. By the way the expression *juvenile offenders* and even *juvenile perpetrators*, that sounds even more debasing was coined, not surprisingly so, by United States law enforcement terminology. And it is among all industrialized Western nations the United States of America that violates most flagrantly the rights of the child in their brutal inhuman and completely paranoid pursuit of punishing children in almost the same ways as they punish adults for simply being natural. This shows, once for all, and *visible* for all, that the glorious nation does not respect the child and that all their rhetoric on child protection is what it is, *empty rhetoric!*

The solutions, in my personal view, for a change of such social, legal and political madness for the better will probably come from a *joint effort of both international and national expert groups* empowered for new policy making, and an effort for open dialogue across the borders of political divergence and cultural diversity.

POSTFACE

The Love Continuum

Who ever thought that problems could be solved by love instead of being well administered by law? Logically so, poets, and lovers, and in a few cases also, lawyers. Very rarely, politicians. Never, the common man.

Love is not a word. It's a universal vibration and energy that is endowed with an intrinsic power! However, most people on this planet do not know love, otherwise we wouldn't suffocate in violence at the four corners of the globe! They may know a shallow concept or concepts they call parental love, passionate love, sexual love or brotherly love, but they don't know *love*.

Love is not the concept called love. The finger pointing to the moon is not the moon.

We spontaneously communicate love through body touch and skin contact, through smile, fondling and caressing, and through abundant eye contact. This is human. Parents fondle and kiss their baby. Lovers embrace each other. Children like to cuddle into their parents' bed and siblings naturally share the same bed until a certain age. Attitudes here vary from one society and one continent to the other, but they vary only a little. There is no educated and emotionally sane human on the globe who would affirm that love can be communicated verbally in any way, or, worse, that love could be defined by language.

Krishnamurti comprehensively explained that love can only be approached negatively, by inquiring in what is *not love*, thereby freeing the mind of the limiting conceptual corset.

Historically, body touch was considered natural; hence it was not reflected upon. And more importantly, it was in no way associated with sexual corruption as it is today in international consumer culture, when a person touches another's naked skin, or an adult a child, or when the two people are co-sleeping naked. When white Americans, Germans,

Austrians or French come to visit Latino or Hispanic cultures, they always wonder how freely in these countries adults touch children. This was observed already in the 1960s when Germans began to visit Italy for holidays, and it has been an ongoing experience since then. And myself being German, I know that Germans have changed, not only their cuisine, but also their way to relate to their children because of exposure to emotionally intelligent cultures.

In olden times, as I know from my mother and grandmother, Germans as good as never touched their children, except for cleaning them or beating them. And when Germans began to travel to Italy, Spain or Greece, they saw that these people abundantly touched their children for pleasure; they saw that both parents and children, most often during dinner time and later in the evening used to be close to each other, the children often sitting on the lap of a parent at dinner, at least for a moment, and that kissing was very much indulged in. *I know that formerly in France and Belgium fathers frequently wet-kissed their prepubescent daughters, while this usually stopped when the girl entered puberty.*

As for mother-son closeness, the privileged moment in these countries is bedtime, when the mother kisses her son on the mouth, and also frequently her daughter, for saying good night. As long as the children are below the school age, parents in these cultures also indulge in taking baths with the children, and nudity may be prolonged for sensuous cuddling in bed or on the sofa for a moment.

During the summer, open-air nudity was common still during my student years in most Mediterranean countries, and even in the French part of Switzerland, between parents and children, and often also when close friends were invited. In Greece and Italy, sensuality assumed always a positive value, and was never depreciated in the way it is in the Anglo-Saxon culture.

In Spain there is lesser body touch than in Italy and Greece. Greece knows since olden times perhaps the most sensual parenting among industrialized nations, and even educators in this country use to touch, fondle and kiss children, except in the upper class.

With the emergence of American-style worldwide television cables to be common in these countries, since about the 1980s, this situation that was very beneficial for emotional intelligence to grow high in children, rapidly decreased and almost disappeared in urban areas. I have observed over the last twenty years in most of Europe, except perhaps Bulgaria, Romania, Georgia and Russia drastic changes in parents relating to their children under the influence of the *insane international media culture* that is dominated by the touch-hostile and paranoid Anglo-American tradition and their life-denying Puritanism.

Interestingly, in Germany, much of the opposite trend has been noticed. As Germans come themselves from an even more touch-denying tradition than Anglo-Saxons, and because they travel so much, and most of the time to Southern Europe, they have adopted much of the sensual attitudes of Italian and Greek parents in relating to their children. In addition, the German media and popular psychology have been outspoken about the damages done to children through early tactile deprivation.

Germans have been more resistant to the touch-hostile messages received during recent years from American-style television series. This led to the result that Germany is by far ahead, compared to

Anglo-Saxon countries, when it's about transiting toward the new educational paradigm of sensual and permissive parenting!

And as an international lawyer, I may speculate that the recent and somehow increasingly stringent political controversy between Germany and the United States on the political arena may have its deeper roots in a *cultural alienation* between Europe and the United States. This really is a matter that concerns values, not just political or economical choices. And when I say *values*, I mean first of all the base values of a culture, such as their educational paradigm, their tolerating, or not, premarital sex, their gender relations, their sex laws, their laws with regard to females' remuneration compared to males,' and last not least ecological values and environmental sensitivity.

Here, the gap between Europe and the United States widens with every year. No politician is politician all the time, no economist looks at their family through the tables of the stock market, and no psychiatrist is looking at their children through the glasses of psychiatry when it's time for cuddling and kissing.

When it's family time, the European parent, at least within the educated strata, and here particularly the male, behaves in a quite different manner than his British or American counterpart. To say it in a somehow simplified manner—as it's of course a very complex matter—I would say that it all boils down to Europe going for less morality and more love, while the United States, Britain, Australia and most of the other Anglo-Saxon countries going for more morality, and less love. And here I am not talking about traditional roles, but about a modern trend, a trend that was to be seen over the last two decades, not earlier. And this despite the America-driven international media culture that is very popular in Germany, France, Italy, Spain or Greece and that may affect the young generations, while in conscious and educated individuals of my generation, there is rather a growing opposition to this kind of highly perverse media culture that focuses only on two topics: money-making and violence!

It is easy to mount a brilliant culture when it's all fake, easy to open a brilliant business when it's all fake. And narcissistic America is the easy show-runner, the fake-of-all-fake specialist. And it's easy to talk in the most eloquent way about love when it's all fake.

In shining America, where all is sunlight and where no shadows are admitted, love and morality are no opposites. For in American culture, love really *is* morality! And here is where they are with one foot in the grave, or in the Middle-Ages. And, by the same token, here is where they have lost any authority, if they ever had any in the first place, to talk about love and abuse or rather what they *think* is love and what they *think* is abuse! For its really a matter of thinking, and not of knowing. Those who know what love is do not talk about it, but they *live their love* and stay away from the very idea to *define love*, or put love in moralistic schemes, or schemes of good behavior, decency, and all the rest of it.

Those who understood the *love continuum* since times immemorial are the natives. And that is why, as a psychological necessity, they attracted the deadly hate of the sadists, the armored Puritans, the righteous crusaders with their phallic rapist's blade. Compulsive sex morality as a concept or lifestyle is unknown to most natives, and it was indeed even unknown to the ancient Chinese sages. It is the bastard of fundamentalism and religious perversion in the form of monotheistic organized religious worship!

Lao-tzu wrote in the *Tao Te Ching* that 'when love is lost, there remains justice, and when justice is lost, there remains ritual'—and I would add, when even rituals are lost, what remains are senseless draconian laws.

In the 42nd verse, Lao-tzu writes that 'sensation bears memory,' which has been confirmed nowadays by neurolinguistic research; hence the importance of sensuality from early in life. In the same verse, Lao-tzu writes 'who loses harmony opposes nature,' and this really is written for the neocolonial arrogant nations of our modern times. And verse 57 bears the solution:

57. CONQUER WITH INACTION

The more morals and taboos there are,
The more cruelty afflicts people;
The more guns and knives there are,
The more factions divide people;
The more arts and skills there are,
The more change obsoletes people;
The more laws and taxes there are,
The more theft corrupts people.

Moralism really is the upside-down movement in life, which transforms the exuberant living structure into dead matter, both outside in the world, and inside, in our bioenergetic setup.

Systemically speaking, this is brought about through the psychological effect of *repression*, which is the immediate response of our biosystem to the prohibition of desire. Repression has several inevitable consequences. These consequences are:

- **1) Regression**
  Regression into more archaic forms of realization of the particular desire that is repressed takes place; this means that for example when sex with children is tabooed and repressed, the normal tender and soft mating game of an adult with a child will be largely replaced by archaic and chaotic forms of sexual conduct, such as violent coercive sex that often is preceded by the secret abduction of the child and that sadly ends in many cases with the murder of the victim;

- **2) Retrogradation**
  Retrogradation of the bioenergetic flux, that is the vital energy contained in the desire will *change its polarity from positive to negative;* this means that the hot and melting sexual feelings will be transformed into bursting urges that need to be abreacted in a more or less explosive manner, or the person will turn into depression

and attract psychosomatic disease; in addition, the positive joyful emotions that accompany sexual mating are transformed into fear, hate and feelings of revenge that, to stay with the example, may be abreacted through a lust for beating the child before raping her, or for torturing the victim during the intercourse;

> **3) Projection**
> Projection, that is what has been repressed and thus was blinded out from consciousness is *projected on others as scapegoats to be punished as a compensation for the forbidden desire.* The practical example here is the notorious lynching and the rape and murder of offenders who are labeled pedophiles, child molesters, baby fuckers, honey fuckers, etc.

It is obvious, while it is often overlooked in psychological publications that repression *directly affects consciousness,* and that it is actually a *shrinking of consciousness* brought about by the morality overlay. I can't imagine something stupider and more conducive to chaos and emotional turmoil than repression. For the modern policy maker, repression as a tool simply is *no-solution;* the whole of human history shows with much evidence where it leads. To stay with our example, it is interesting in this context to note that in former epochs, when sex laws were either non-existent or not harshly enforced, there was a much higher occurrence of adult-child sexual interaction than today in modern nations, but the number of children being abducted and murdered for sexual reasons was relatively low, if not nonexistent. And we have proof to the contrary during epochs that were even more repressive as our present day Anglo-Saxon countries, that is the period of early Puritanism in England and the era of Calvinism in the *Suisse Romande*, especially Lausanne and Geneva, which were infamous for their high incidence of both 'educational' child assault, torture and murder, and for their high incidence of violent child rape and murder. What we can learn from these historical examples is that repression does not serve a rational goal in that it does not prevent crime, but in the contrary leads to *more crime.*

Other notorious examples for the counterproductive and chaotic effects of repression are the *Prohibition* in the United States, Russia and the more spectacular death toll during the alcohol prohibition in Iran during the regime of the Ayatollah Khomeini.

Repression leads to compensatory satisfactions, which are always bad solutions. The high death toll especially during the enforced alcohol prohibition in Iran was due to the high amounts of methanol (airplane fuel) consumed as a replacement for the forbidden alcoholic beverage.

Regarding the repression of sexual desire it is since long known that one of the most frequent compensatory reactions for forbidden pleasure is violence, most often in the form of *beatings given to the sexual mate* either before mating or during the mating game, or both. It has been found that the serial child murderer Jürgen Bartsch admitted in one of his journals that originally *he did not want to murder children,* but desired them sexually. This was back in his adolescence.

As Bartsch was an orphan and grew up in an extremely repressive host family, and was frequently beaten by the couple who adopted him, he thought that 'nobody could love him' while he reported one incidence of a little boy kissing him on the mouth when he met with the boy in a forest, a fact Bartsch could not believe. At that time, Bartsch's activities with smaller boys were a ritual in which Bartsch would undress the boy and then give him a beating on the naked bottom. It was during this ritual that the boy kissed him and thus signaled him his love and devotion. But Bartsch could not believe anybody in the world could love him, as his selflove was virtually nonexistent. As a result, his sexual perversion took on more violent forms once he was grown up, and the sexual torture he was then inflicting upon male children he met led to the death of several boys.

This does not seem surprising after all, from an energy point of view of view. The energies we disown turn against us. There is about no better evidence for the fact that repressing child-adult sexual interaction leads to more sexual crime against children! And yet, in a society that has lost its natural love continuum what is the natural solution seems anathema to the policy makers. In fact, sex has many healing properties, as wine does.

And there is a *natural correlation* of the repression of sex and the repression of wine. Wine was a wisdom drink since times immemorial. The ancient Greek immortalized wine by assigning a God to wine, Dionysus, who was the god of ebriety that the Romans later called Bacchus.

Already long before, the ancient Chinese and the Tibetans sanctified ebriety as a godly quality, similar to the state right after orgasm, which is considered in many polytheistic religions as a purely religious state. Many of the old traditional poems of ancient China and Tibet were written by their poets in a state of ebriety that was inspired and that was considered a privilege for the sage, while ebriety with ordinary people was considered a sign of vulgarity.

To throw wine in one pot with all strong alcohol and talk about 'alcoholic beverages' only betrays the ignorance of the culture that throws such misnomers around in the public health discussion. Quite recently, in 2004, in France, a scientific study was undertaken that showed the many healing properties of wine, which was of course only published in France and met only mute silence in all Anglo-Saxon countries. The same is true for sex. Sigmund Freud, during the first years of the 20th century, showed the sexual etiology of all neuroses, and this is now established psychiatric knowledge, and was largely confirmed and expanded by Wilhelm Reich, Alexander Lowen, and others.

This means in clear text that the natural streaming of sexual energy heals neurosis. Even before Reich, this was known to bioenergy researchers such as Paracelsus and Mesmer. Beyond this, alternative psychiatrists such as Ronald David Laing, one of the founders of *antipsychiatry* in England, found that when schizophrenic youngsters are led to experience sex without anxiety and repression, their schizophrenia vanishes in a period ranging from several weeks to several months.

This is so much the more surprising as schizophrenia was held by mainstream psychiatry as absolutely incurable for centuries in a row, a view that was first questioned and invalidated by Carl Jung, but only proven clinically by Wilhelm Reich.

—Carl-Gustav Jung, On the Psychogenesis of Schizophrenia (1993), pp. 474-475 and Wilhelm Reich, The Schizophrenic Split (1945).

BIBLIOGRAPHY

Contextual Bibliography

ABRAMS, JEREMIAH (ED.)

Reclaiming the Inner Child
NEW YORK: TARCHER/PUTNAM, 1990

ALSTON, JOHN P. / TUCKER, FRANCIS

The Myth of Sexual Permissiveness
THE JOURNAL OF SEX RESEARCH, 9/1 (1973)

APPLETON, MATTHEW

A Free Range Childhood
SELF-REGULATION AT SUMMERHILL SCHOOL
FOUNDATION FOR EDUCATIONAL RENEWAL, 2000

ARCAS, GÉRALD, DR

Guérir le corps par l'hypnose et l'auto-hypnose
PARIS: SAND, 1997

ARIÈS, PHILIPPE

L'enfant et la famille sous l'Ancien Régime
PARIS, SEUIL, 1975

Centuries of Childhood
NEW YORK: VINTAGE BOOKS, 1962

Geschichte der Kindheit
FRANKFURT/M: DTV, 1998

ARNTZ, WILLIAM & CHASSE, BETSY

What the Bleep Do We Know
20TH CENTURY FOX, 2005 (DVD)

Down The Rabbit Hole Quantum Edition
20TH CENTURY FOX, 2006 (3 DVD SET)

Relationships and Life Cycles
ASTROLOGICAL PATTERNS OF PERSONAL EXPERIENCE
SEBASTOPOL, CA: CRCS PUBLICATIONS, 1993

ATLEE, TOM

The Tao of Democracy
USING CO-INTELLIGENCE TO CREATE A WORLD THAT WORKS FOR ALL
NORTH CHARLESTON, SC: IMPRINT BOOKS / WORLDWORKS PRESS, 2003

BACHELARD, GASTON

The Poetics of Reverie
BOSTON: BEACON PRESS, 1971

BIBLIOGRAPHY

BAGGINS, DAVID SADOFSKY

Drug Hate and the Corruption of American Justice
SANTA BARBARA: PRAEGER, 1998

BAGLEY, CHRISTOPHER

Child Abusers
RESEARCH AND TREATMENT
NEW YORK: UNIVERSAL PUBLISHERS, 2003

BALTER, MICHAEL

The Goddess and the Bull
CATALHOYUK, AN ARCHAEOLOGICAL JOURNEY
TO THE DAWN OF CIVILIZATION
NEW YORK: FREE PRESS, 2006

BANDLER, RICHARD

Get the Life You Want
THE SECRETS TO QUICK AND LASTING LIFE CHANGE
WITH NEURO-LINGUISTIC PROGRAMMING
DEERFIELD BEACH, FL: HCI, 2008

BARBAREE, HOWARD E. & MARSHALL, WILLIAM L.
(EDS.)

The Juvenile Sex Offender
SECOND EDITION
NEW YORK: GUILFORD PRESS, 2008

BARRON, FRANK X., MONTUORI, ET AL. (EDS.)

Creators on Creating
AWAKENING AND CULTIVATING THE IMAGINATIVE MIND
(NEW CONSCIOUSNESS READER)
NEW YORK: P. TARCHER/PUTNAM, 1997

BATESON, GREGORY

Steps to an Ecology of Mind
CHICAGO: UNIVERSITY OF CHICAGO PRESS, 2000
ORIGINALLY PUBLISHED IN 1972

BENDER LAURETTA & BLAU, ABRAM

The Reaction of Children to Sexual Relations with Adults
AMERICAN J. ORTHOPSYCHIATRY 7 (1937), 500-518

BENKLER, YOCHAI

The Wealth of Networks
HOW SOCIAL PRODUCTION TRANSFORMS MARKETS AND FREEDOM
NEW HAVEN, CT: YALE UNIVERSITY PRESS, 2007

BENNION, FRANCIS

Statutory Interpretation
LONDON: BUTTERWORTHS, 1984

BERNARD, FRITS

Paedophilia
A FACTUAL REPORT
AMSTERDAM: ENCLAVE, 1985

BERTALANFFY, LUDWIG VON

General Systems Theory
FOUNDATIONS, DEVELOPMENT, APPLICATIONS
NEW YORK: GEORGE BRAZILIER PUBLISHING, 1976

BESANT, ANNIE

An Autobiography
NEW DELHI: PENGUIN BOOKS, 2005
ORIGINALLY PUBLISHED IN 1893

BETTELHEIM, BRUNO

A Good Enough Parent
NEW YORK: A. KNOPF, 1987

The Uses of Enchantment
NEW YORK: VINTAGE BOOKS, 1989

BOHM, DAVID

Wholeness and the Implicate Order
LONDON: ROUTLEDGE, 2002

Thought as a System
LONDON: ROUTLEDGE, 1994

Quantum Theory
LONDON: DOVER PUBLICATIONS, 1989

BOLDT, LAURENCE G.

Zen and the Art of Making a Living
A PRACTICAL GUIDE TO CREATIVE CAREER DESIGN
NEW YORK: PENGUIN ARKANA, 1993

How to Find the Work You Love
NEW YORK: PENGUIN ARKANA, 1996

Zen Soup
TASTY MORSELS OF ZEN WISDOM FROM GREAT MINDS EAST & WEST
NEW YORK: PENGUIN ARKANA, 1997

The Tao of Abundance
EIGHT ANCIENT PRINCIPLES FOR ABUNDANT LIVING
NEW YORK: PENGUIN ARKANA, 1999

BORDEAUX-SZEKELY, EDMOND

Teaching of the Essenes from Enoch to the Dead
SEA SCROLLS
BEEKMAN PUBLISHING, 1992

Gospel of the Essenes
THE UNKNOWN BOOKS OF THE ESSENES
& LOST SCROLLS OF THE ESSENE BROTHERHOOD
BEEKMAN PUBLISHING, 1988

Gospel of Peace of Jesus Christ
BEEKMAN PUBLISHING, 1994

Gospel of Peace, 2d Vol.
I B S INTERNATIONAL PUBLISHERS

BRANDEN, NATHANIEL

How to Raise Your Self-Esteem
NEW YORK: BANTAM, 1987

BRANT & TISZA

The Sexually Misused Child
AMERICAN J. ORTHOPSYCHIATRY, 47(1)(1977)

BRASSAI

Conversations with Picasso
CHICAGO: UNIVERSITY OF CHICAGO PUBLICATIONS, 1999

BRENNAN, BARBARA ANN

Hands of Healing
A GUIDE TO HEALING THROUGH THE HUMAN ENERGY FIELD
NEW YORK: BANTAM, 1988

BRONGERSMA, EDWARD

Aggression against Pedophiles
7 INTERNATIONAL JOURNAL OF LAW & PSYCHIATRY 82 (1984)

Loving Boys
AMSTERDAM, NEW YORK: GAP, 1987

BRUCE, ALEXANDRA

Beyond the Bleep
THE DEFINITE UNAUTHORIZED GUIDE TO 'WHAT THE BLEEP DO WE KNOW!?'
NEW YORK: DISINFORMATION, 2005

BULLOUGH & BULLOUGH (EDS.)

Human Sexuality
AN ENCYCLOPEDIA
NEW YORK: GARLAND PUBLISHING, 1994

Sin, Sickness and Sanity
A HISTORY OF SEXUAL ATTITUDES
NEW YORK: NEW AMERICAN LIBRARY, 1977

BURGESS, ANN WOLBERT

Child Pornography and Sex Rings
NEW YORK: LEXINGTON BOOKS, 1984

BURWICK, FREDERICK

The Damnation of Newton
GOETHE'S COLOR THEORY AND ROMANTIC PERCEPTION
NEW YORK: WALTER DE GRUYTER, 1986

BIBLIOGRAPHY

Butler-Bowden, Tom

50 Success Classics
Winning Wisdom for Work & Life From 50 Landmark Books
London: Nicholas Brealey Publishing, 2004

Buxton, Richard

The Complete World of Greek Mythology
London: Thames & Hudson, 2007

Cain, Chelsea & Moon Unit Zappa

Wild Child
New York: Seal Press (Feminist Publishing), 1999

Calderone & Ramey

Talking With Your Child About Sex
New York: Random House, 1982

Campbell, Herbert James

The Pleasure Areas
London: Eyre Methuen Ltd., 1973

Campbell, Jacqueline C.

Assessing Dangerousness
Violence by Sexual Offenders, Batterers and Child

Abusers
New York: Sage Publications, 2004

Campbell, Joseph

The Hero With A Thousand Faces
Princeton: Princeton University Press, 1973
(Bollingen Series XVII)
London: Orion Books, 1999

Occidental Mythology
Princeton: Princeton University Press, 1973
(Bollingen Series XVII)
New York: Penguin Arkana, 1991

The Masks of God
Oriental Mythology
New York: Penguin Arkana, 1992
Originally published 1962

The Power of Myth
With Bill Moyers
ed. by Sue Flowers
New York: Anchor Books, 1988

Capacchione, Lucia

The Power of Your Other Hand
North Hollywood, CA: Newcastle Publishing, 1988

BIBLIOGRAPHY

CAPRA, BERNT AMADEUS

Mindwalk
A FILM FOR PASSIONATE THINKERS
BASED UPON FRITJOF CAPRA'S THE TURNING POINT
NEW YORK: TRITON PICTURES, 1990

CAPRA, FRITJOF

The Turning Point
SCIENCE, SOCIETY AND THE RISING CULTURE
NEW YORK: SIMON & SCHUSTER, 1987
ORIGINAL AUTHOR COPYRIGHT, 1982

The Tao of Physics
AN EXPLORATION OF THE PARALLELS BETWEEN MODERN
PHYSICS AND EASTERN MYSTICISM
NEW YORK: SHAMBHALA PUBLICATIONS, 2000
(NEW EDITION) ORIGINALLY PUBLISHED IN 1975

The Web of Life
A NEW SCIENTIFIC UNDERSTANDING OF LIVING SYSTEMS
NEW YORK: DOUBLEDAY, 1997
AUTHOR COPYRIGHT 1996

The Hidden Connections
INTEGRATING THE BIOLOGICAL, COGNITIVE AND SOCIAL
DIMENSIONS OF LIFE INTO A SCIENCE OF SUSTAINABILITY
NEW YORK: DOUBLEDAY, 2002

Steering Business Toward Sustainability
NEW YORK: UNITED NATIONS UNIVERSITY PRESS, 1995

Uncommon Wisdom
CONVERSATIONS WITH REMARKABLE PEOPLE
NEW YORK: BANTAM, 1989

The Science of Leonardo
INSIDE THE MIND OF THE GREAT GENIUS OF THE RENAISSANCE
NEW YORK: ANCHOR BOOKS, 2008
NEW YORK: BANTAM DOUBLEDAY, 2007 (FIRST PUBLISHING)

COMPLETE LIST OF PUBLICATIONS
HTTP://WWW.FRITJOFCAPRA.NET/PUBLISHERS.HTML

CASSOU, MICHELLE & CUBLEY, STEWARD

Life, Paint and Passion
RECLAIMING THE MAGIC OF SPONTANEOUS EXPRESSION
NEW YORK: P. TARCHER/PUTNAM, 1996

CASTANEDA, CARLOS

The Teachings of Don Juan
A YAQUI WAY OF KNOWLEDGE
WASHINGTON: SQUARE PRESS, 1985

Journey to Ixtlan
WASHINGTON: SQUARE PRESS: 1991

Tales of Power
WASHINGTON: SQUARE PRESS, 1991

The Second Ring of Power
WASHINGTON: SQUARE PRESS, 1991

CLARKE-STEWARD, S., FRIEDMAN, S. & KOCH, J.

Child Development, A Topical Approach
LONDON: JOHN WILEY, 1986

CONSTANTINE, LARRY L.

Children & Sex
NEW FINDINGS, NEW PERSPECTIVES
LARRY L. CONSTANTINE & FLOYD M. MARTINSON (EDS.)
BOSTON: LITTLE, BROWN & COMPANY, 1981

Treasures of the Island
CHILDREN IN ALTERNATIVE LIFESTYLES
BEVERLY HILLS: SAGE PUBLICATIONS, 1976

Where are the Kids?
IN: LIBBY & WHITEHURST (ED.)
MARRIAGE AND ALTERNATIVES
GLENVIEW: SCOTT FORESMAN, 1977

Open Family
A LIFESTYLE FOR KIDS AND OTHER PEOPLE
26 FAMILY COORDINATOR 113-130 (1977)

COOK, M. & HOWELLS, K. (EDS.)

Adult Sexual Interest in Children
ACADEMIC PRESS, LONDON, 1980

COVITZ, JOEL

Emotional Child Abuse
THE FAMILY CURSE
BOSTON: SIGO PRESS, 1986

CURRIER, RICHARD L.

Juvenile Sexuality in Global Perspective
IN : CHILDREN & SEX, NEW FINDINGS, NEW PERSPECTIVES
LARRY L. CONSTANTINE & FLOYD M. MARTINSON (EDS.)
BOSTON: LITTLE, BROWN & COMPANY, 1981

DALAI LAMA

Ethics for the New Millennium
NEW YORK: PENGUIN PUTNAM, 1999

DAVIS, A. J.

Sexual Assaults in the Philadelphia Prison System and Sheriff's Van
TRANS-ACTION 6, 2, 8-16 (1968)

DEAN & BRUYN-KOPS

The Crime and the Consequences of Rape
NEW YORK: THOMAS, 1982

DE BONO, EDWARD

The Use of Lateral Thinking
NEW YORK: PENGUIN, 1967

The Mechanism of Mind
NEW YORK: PENGUIN, 1969

Sur/Petition
LONDON: HARPERCOLLINS, 1993

Tactics
LONDON: HARPERCOLLINS, 1993
FIRST PUBLISHED IN 1985

Serious Creativity
USING THE POWER OF LATERAL THINKING TO CREATE NEW IDEAS
LONDON: HARPERCOLLINS, 1996

DELACOUR, JEAN-BAPTISTE

Glimpses of the Beyond
NEW YORK: BANTAM DELL, 1975

DEMAUSE, LLOYD

The History of Childhood
NEW YORK, 1974

Foundations of Psychohistory
NEW YORK: CREATIVE ROOTS, 1982

DIAMOND, STEPHEN A., MAY, ROLLO

Anger, Madness, and the Daimonic
THE PSYCHOLOGICAL GENESIS OF VIOLENCE, EVIL AND CREATIVITY
NEW YORK: STATE UNIVERSITY OF NEW YORK PRESS, 1999

DiCARLO, RUSSELL E. (ED.)

Towards A New World View
CONVERSATIONS AT THE LEADING EDGE
ERIE, PA: EPIC PUBLISHING, 1996

DOLTO, FRANÇOISE

La Cause des Enfants
PARIS: LAFFONT, 1985

Psychanalyse et Pédiatrie
PARIS: SEUIL, 1971

Séminaire de Psychanalyse d'Enfants, 1
PARIS: SEUIL, 1982

Séminaire de Psychanalyse d'Enfants, 2
PARIS: SEUIL, 1985

Séminaire de Psychanalyse d'Enfants, 3
PARIS: SEUIL, 1988

L'évangile au risque de la psychanalyse
PARIS: SEUIL, 1980

BIBLIOGRAPHY

Dürckheim, Karlfried Graf

Hara: The Vital Center of Man
Rochester: Inner Traditions, 2004

Zen and Us
New York: Penguin Arkana 1991

The Call for the Master
New York: Penguin Books, 1993

Absolute Living
The Otherworldly in the World and the Path to Maturity
New York: Penguin Arkana, 1992

The Way of Transformation
Daily Life as a Spiritual Exercise
London: Allen & Unwin, 1988

The Japanese Cult of Tranquility
London: Rider, 1960

Eden, Donna & Feinstein, David

Energy Medicine
New York: Tarcher/Putnam, 1998

The Energy Medicine Kit
Simple Effective Techniques to Help You Boost Your Vitality
Boulder, Co.: Sounds True Editions, 2004

The Promise of Energy Psychology
With David Feinstein and Gary Craig
Revolutionary Tools for Dramatic Personal Change
New York: Jeremy P. Tarcher/Penguin, 2005

EDMUNDS, FRANCIS

An Introduction to Anthroposophy
RUDOLF STEINER'S WORLDVIEW
LONDON: RUDOLF STEINER PRESS, 2005

EDWARDES, A.

The Jewel of the Lotus
NEW YORK, 1959

EINSTEIN, ALBERT

The World As I See It
NEW YORK: CITADEL PRESS, 1993

Out of My Later Years
NEW YORK: OUTLET, 1993

Ideas and Opinions
NEW YORK: BONANZA BOOKS, 1988

Albert Einstein Notebook
LONDON: DOVER PUBLICATIONS, 1989

EISLER, RIANE

The Chalice and the Blade
OUR HISTORY, OUR FUTURE
SAN FRANCISCO: HARPER & ROW, 1995

Sacred Pleasure: Sex, Myth and the Politics of the Body
NEW PATHS TO POWER AND LOVE

BIBLIOGRAPHY

SAN FRANCISCO: HARPER & ROW, 1996

The Partnership Way
NEW TOOLS FOR LIVING AND LEARNING
WITH DAVID LOYE
BRANDON, VT: HOLISTIC EDUCATION PRESS, 1998

ELWIN, V.

The Muria and their Ghotul
BOMBAY: OXFORD UNIVERSITY PRESS, 1947

The Secret Life of Water
NEW YORK: ATRIA BOOKS, 2005

ERICKSON, MILTON H.

My Voice Will Go With You
THE TEACHING TALES OF MILTON H. ERICKSON
BY SIDNEY ROSEN (ED.)
NEW YORK: NORTON & CO., 1991

Complete Works 1.0, CD-ROM
NEW YORK: MILTON H. ERICKSON FOUNDATION, 2001

ERIKSON, ERIK H.

Childhood and Society
NEW YORK: NORTON, 1993
FIRST PUBLISHED IN 1950

FARSON, RICHARD

Birthrights
A BILL OF RIGHTS FOR CHILDREN
MACMILLAN, NEW YORK, 1974

FEINBERG, JOEL

Harmless Wrongdoing
THE MORAL LIMITS OF THE CRIMINAL LAW, VOL. 4
NEW YORK: OXFORD UNIVERSITY PRESS, 1990

FENSTERHALM, HERBERT

Don't Say Yes When You Want to Say No
WITH JEAN BEAR
NEW YORK: DELL, 1980

FINKELHOR, DAVID

Sexually Victimized Children
NEW YORK: FREE PRESS, 1981

FINKELSTEIN, HAIM N. (ED.)

The Collected Writings of Salvador Dali
CAMBRIDGE: CAMBRIDGE UNIVERSITY PRESS, 1998

BIBLIOGRAPHY

FORTUNE, MARY M.

Sexual Violence
NEW YORK: PILGRIM PRESS, 1994

FOSTER/FREED

A Bill of Rights for Children
6 FAMILY LAW QUARTERLY 343 (1972)

FOUCAULT, MICHEL

The History of Sexuality, Vol. I : The Will to Knowledge
LONDON: PENGUIN, 1998
FIRST PUBLISHED IN 1976

The History of Sexuality, Vol. II : The Use of Pleasure
LONDON: PENGUIN, 1998
FIRST PUBLISHED IN 1984

The History of Sexuality, Vol. III : The Care of Self
LONDON: PENGUIN, 1998
FIRST PUBLISHED IN 1984

FREUD, SIGMUND

Three Essays on the Theory of Sexuality
IN: THE STANDARD EDITION OF THE COMPLETE PSYCHOLOGICAL
WORKS OF SIGMUND FREUD
LONDON: HOGARTH PRESS, 1953-54
VOL. 7, PP. 130 FF
(FIRST PUBLISHED IN 1905)

The Interpretation of Dreams
NEW YORK: AVON, REISSUE EDITION, 1980
AND IN: THE STANDARD EDITION OF THE COMPLETE PSYCHOLOGICAL
WORKS OF SIGMUND FREUD , (24 VOLUMES) ED. BY JAMES STRACHEY
NEW YORK: W. W. NORTON & COMPANY, 1976

Totem and Taboo
NEW YORK: ROUTLEDGE, 1999
ORIGINALLY PUBLISHED IN 1913

FREUND, KURT

Assessment of Pedophilia
IN: COOK, M. AND HOWELLS, K. (EDS.)
ADULT SEXUAL INTEREST IN CHILDREN
ACADEMIC PRESS, LONDON, 1980

FROMM, ERICH

The Anatomy of Human Destructiveness
NEW YORK: OWL BOOK, 1992
ORIGINALLY PUBLISHED IN 1973

Escape from Freedom
NEW YORK: OWL BOOKS, 1994
ORIGINALLY PUBLISHED IN 1941

TO HAVE OR TO BE
NEW YORK: CONTINUUM INTERNATIONAL PUBLISHING, 1996
ORIGINALLY PUBLISHED IN 1976

The Art of Loving
NEW YORK: HARPERPERENNIAL, 2000
ORIGINALLY PUBLISHED IN 1956

GELDARD, RICHARD

Remembering Heraclitus
NEW YORK: LINDISFARNE BOOKS, 2000

GERBER, RICHARD

A Practical Guide to Vibrational Medicine
ENERGY HEALING AND SPIRITUAL TRANSFORMATION
NEW YORK: HARPER & COLLINS, 2001

GELLER, URI

The Mindpower Kit
INCLUDES BOOK, AUDIOTAPE, QUARTZ CRYSTAL AND MEDITATION
CIRCLE
NEW YORK: PENGUIN, 1996

GESELL, IZZY

Playing Along
37 GROUP LEARNING ACTIVITIES BORROWED FROM IMPROVISATIONAL
THEATER
WHOLE PERSON ASSOCIATES, 1997

GHISELIN, BREWSTER (ED.)

The Creative Process
REFLECTIONS ON INVENTION IN THE ARTS AND SCIENCES
BERKELEY: UNIVERSITY OF CALIFORNIA PRESS, 1985
FIRST PUBLISHED IN 1952

GIBSON, IAN

The Shameful Life of Salvador Dali
NEW YORK: NORTON, 1998

GIL, DAVID G.

Societal Violence and Violence in Families
IN: DAVID G. GIL, CHILD ABUSE AND VIOLENCE
NEW YORK: AMS PRESS, 1928

GIMBUTAS, MARIJA

The Language of the Goddess
LONDON: THAMES & HUDSON, 2001

GOLDENSTEIN, JOYCE

Einstein: Physicist and Genius
(GREAT MINDS OF SCIENCE)
NEW YORK: ENSLOW PUBLISHERS, 1995

GOLDMAN, JONATHAN & GOLDMAN, ANDI

Tantra of Sound
FREQUENCIES OF HEALING
CHARLOTTESVILLE: HAMPTON ROADS, 2005

Healing Sounds
THE POWER OF HARMONIES
ROCHESTER: HEALING ARTS PRESS, 2002

Healing Sounds
PRINCIPLES OF SOUND HEALING
DVD, 90 MIN.
SACRED MYSTERIES, 2004

GOLDSTEIN, JEFFREY H.

Aggression and Crimes of Violence
NEW YORK, 1975

GOLEMAN, DANIEL

Emotional Intelligence
NEW YORK, BANTAM BOOKS, 1995

GORDON, ROSEMARY

Pedophilia: Normal and Abnormal
IN: KRAEMER, THE FORBIDDEN LOVE
LONDON, 1976

GORDON WASSON, R.

The Road to Eleusis
UNVEILING THE SECRET OF THE MYSTERIES
WITH ALBERT HOFMANN, HUSTON SMITH, CARL RUCK AND PETER WEBSTER
BERKELEY, CA: NORTH ATLANTIC BOOKS, 2008

GOSWAMI, AMIT

The Self-Aware Universe
HOW CONSCIOUSNESS CREATES THE MATERIAL WORLD
NEW YORK: TARCHER/PUTNAM, 1995

GOTTLIEB, ADAM

Peyote and Other Psychoactive Cacti
RONIN PUBLISHING, 2ND EDITION, 1997

GREENE, LIZ

Astrology of Fate
YORK BEACH, ME: RED WHEEL/WEISER, 1986

Saturn
A NEW LOOK AT AN OLD DEVIL
YORK BEACH, ME: RED WHEEL/WEISER, 1976

The Astrological Neptune and the Quest for Redemption
BOSTON: RED WHEEL WEISER, 1996

The Mythic Journey
WITH JULIET SHARMAN-BURKE
THE MEANING OF MYTH AS A GUIDE FOR LIFE
NEW YORK: SIMON & SCHUSTER (FIRESIDE), 2000

The Mythic Tarot
WITH JULIET SHARMAN-BURKE
NEW YORK: SIMON & SCHUSTER (FIRESIDE), 2001
ORIGINALLY PUBLISHED IN 1986

The Luminaries
THE PSYCHOLOGY OF THE SUN AND MOON IN THE HOROSCOPE
WITH HOWARD SASPORTAS
YORK BEACH, ME: RED WHEEL/WEISER, 1992

GREER, JOHN MICHAEL

Earth Divination, Earth Magic
A PRACTICAL GUIDE TO GEOMANCY
NEW YORK: LLEWELLYN PUBLICATIONS, 1999

GROF, STANISLAV

Ancient Wisdom and Modern Science
NEW YORK: STATE UNIVERSITY OF NEW YORK PRESS, 1984

Beyond the Brain
BIRTH, DEATH AND TRANSCENDENCE IN PSYCHOTHERAPY
NEW YORK: STATE UNIVERSITY OF NEW YORK, 1985

LSD: Doorway to the Numinous
THE GROUNDBREAKING PSYCHEDELIC RESEARCH INTO REALMS OF THE
HUMAN UNCONSCIOUS

Rochester: Park Street Press, 2009

Realms of the Human Unconscious
Observations from LSD Research
New York: E.P. Dutton, 1976

The Cosmic Game
Explorations of the Frontiers of Human Consciousness
New York: State University of New York Press, 1998

The Holotropic Mind
The Three Levels of Human Consciousness
With Hal Zina Bennett
New York: HarperCollins, 1993

When the Impossible Happens
Adventures in Non-Ordinary Reality
Louisville, CO: Sounds True, 2005

Groth, A. Nicholas

Men Who Rape
The Psychology of the Offender
New York: Perseus Publishing, 1980

Holmes, Ernst

The Science of Mind
A Philosophy, A Faith, A Way of Life
New York: Jeremy P. Tarcher/Putnam, 1998
First Published in 1938

HOOD, J. X.

Scientific Curiosities of Love, Sex and Marriage
A SURVEY OF SEX RELATIONS, BELIEFS AND CUSTOMS OF MANKIND IN DIFFERENT COUNTRIES AND AGES
NEW YORK, 1951

HOUSTON, JEAN

The Possible Human
A COURSE IN ENHANCING YOUR PHYSICAL, MENTAL, AND CREATIVE ABILITIES
NEW YORK: JEREMY P. TARCHER/PUTNAM, 1982

HOWELLS, KEVIN

Adult Sexual Interest in Children
CONSIDERATIONS RELEVANT TO THEORIES OF AETIOLOGY IN:
COOK, M. AND HOWELLS, K. (EDS.): ADULT SEXUAL INTEREST IN CHILDREN
ACADEMIC PRESS, LONDON, 1980

HUANG, ALFRED

The Complete I Ching
THE DEFINITE TRANSLATION FROM TAOIST MASTER ALFRED HUANG
ROCHESTER, NY: INNER TRADITIONS, 1998

HUNT, VALERIE

Infinite Mind
SCIENCE OF THE HUMAN VIBRATIONS OF CONSCIOUSNESS
MALIBU, CA: MALIBU PUBLISHING, 2000

INNOCENTI DECLARATION

Declaration on the Protection, Promotion and Support of Breastfeeding
HTTP://WWW.INNOCENTI15.NET/INNO.HTM

JACKSON, NIGEL

The Rune Mysteries
WITH SILVER RAVENWOLF
ST. PAUL, MINN.: LLEWELLYN PUBLICATIONS, 2000

JACKSON, STEVI

Childhood and Sexuality
NEW YORK: BLACKWELL, 1982

JAFFE, HANS L.C.

Picasso
NEW YORK: ABRADALE PRESS, 1996

BIBLIOGRAPHY

JAMES, WILLIAM

Writings 1902-1910
THE VARIETIES OF RELIGIOUS EXPERIENCE / PRAGMATISM / A PLURALISTIC
UNIVERSE / THE MEANING OF TRUTH / SOME PROBLEMS OF PHILOSOPHY / ESSAYS
NEW YORK: LIBRARY OF AMERICA, 1988

JANOV, ARTHUR

Primal Man
THE NEW CONSCIOUSNESS
NEW YORK: CROWELL, 1975

JOHNSON, PAUL

A History of the Jews
NEW YORK: HARPER & ROW, 1987

JOHNSTON & DEISHER

Contemporary Communal Child Rearing: A First Analysis
52 PEDIATRICS 319 (1973)

JONES, W.H.S., LITT, D.

Pliny Natural History
CAMBRIDGE, MASS.: HARVARD UNIVERSITY PRESS, 1980

JUNG, CARL GUSTAV

Archetypes of the Collective Unconscious
IN: THE BASIC WRITINGS OF C.G. JUNG
NEW YORK: THE MODERN LIBRARY, 1959, 358-407

Collected Works
NEW YORK, 1959

On the Nature of the Psyche
IN: THE BASIC WRITINGS OF C.G. JUNG
NEW YORK: THE MODERN LIBRARY, 1959, 47-133

Psychological Types
COLLECTED WRITINGS, VOL. 6
PRINCETON: PRINCETON UNIVERSITY PRESS, 1971

Psychology and Religion
IN: THE BASIC WRITINGS OF C.G. JUNG
NEW YORK: THE MODERN LIBRARY, 1959, 582-655

Religious and Psychological Problems of Alchemy
IN: THE BASIC WRITINGS OF C.G. JUNG
NEW YORK: THE MODERN LIBRARY, 1959, 537-581

Symbol und Libido
FREIBURG: WALTER VERLAG, 1987

The Basic Writings of C.G. Jung
NEW YORK: THE MODERN LIBRARY, 1959

The Development of Personality
COLLECTED WRITINGS, VOL. 17
PRINCETON: PRINCETON UNIVERSITY PRESS, 1954

The Meaning and Significance of Dreams
BOSTON: SIGO PRESS, 1991

The Myth of the Divine Child
IN: ESSAYS ON A SCIENCE OF MYTHOLOGY
PRINCETON, N.J.: PRINCETON UNIVERSITY PRESS BOLLINGEN
SERIES XXII, 1969. (WITH KARL KERENYI)

Two Essays on Analytical Psychology
COLLECTED WRITINGS, VOL. 7
PRINCETON: PRINCETON UNIVERSITY PRESS, 1972
FIRST PUBLISHED BY ROUTLEDGE & KEGAN PAUL, LTD., 1953

KAHN, CHARLES (ED.)

The Art and Thought of Heraclitus
CAMBRIDGE: CAMBRIDGE UNIVERSITY PRESS, 2008

KAPLEAU, ROSHI PHILIP

Three Pillars of Zen
BOSTON: BEACON PRESS, 1967

KARAGULLA, SHAFICA

The Chakras
CORRELATIONS BETWEEN MEDICAL SCIENCE AND CLAIRVOYANT
OBSERVATION (WITH DORA VAN GELDER KUNZ)
WHEATON: QUEST BOOKS, 1989

KLEIN, MELANIE

Love, Guilt and Reparation, and Other Works 1921-1945
NEW YORK: FREE PRESS, 1984

(REISSUE EDITION)

Envy and Gratitude and Other Works 1946-1963
NEW YORK: FREE PRESS, 2002
(REISSUE EDITION)

KOESTLER, ARTHUR

The Act of Creation
NEW YORK: PENGUIN ARKANA, 1989.
ORIGINALLY PUBLISHED IN 1964

KRAEMER

The Forbidden Love
LONDON, 1976

KRAFFT-EBING, RICHARD VON

Psychopathia sexualis
NEW YORK: BELL PUBLISHING, 1965
ORIGINALLY PUBLISHED IN 1886

KRAUSE, DONALD G.

The Art of War for Executives
LONDON: NICHOLAS BREALEY PUBLISHING, 1995

KRISHNAMURTI, J.

Freedom From The Known
SAN FRANCISCO: HARPER & ROW, 1969

The First and Last Freedom
SAN FRANCISCO: HARPER & ROW, 1975

Education and the Significance of Life
LONDON: VICTOR GOLLANCZ, 1978

Commentaries on Living
FIRST SERIES
LONDON: VICTOR GOLLANCZ, 1985

Commentaries on Living
SECOND SERIES
LONDON: VICTOR GOLLANCZ, 1986

Krishnamurti's Journal
LONDON: VICTOR GOLLANCZ, 1987

Krishnamurti's Notebook
LONDON: VICTOR GOLLANCZ, 1986

Beyond Violence
LONDON: VICTOR GOLLANCZ, 1985

Beginnings of Learning
NEW YORK: PENGUIN, 1986

The Penguin Krishnamurti Reader
NEW YORK: PENGUIN, 1987

On God
SAN FRANCISCO: HARPER & ROW, 1992

On Fear
SAN FRANCISCO: HARPER & ROW, 1995

The Essential Krishnamurti
SAN FRANCISCO: HARPER & ROW, 1996

The Ending of Time
WITH DR. DAVID BOHM
SAN FRANCISCO: HARPER & ROW, 1985

LAING, RONALD DAVID

Divided Self
NEW YORK: VIKING PRESS, 1991

R.D. Laing and the Paths of Anti-Psychiatry
ED., BY Z. KOTOWICZ
LONDON: ROUTLEDGE, 1997

The Politics of Experience
NEW YORK: PANTHEON, 1983

LAKHOVSKY, GEORGES

Secret of Life
NEW YORK: KESSINGER PUBLISHING, 2003

LASZLO, ERVIN

Science and the Akashic Field
AN INTEGRAL THEORY OF EVERYTHING
ROCHESTER: INNER TRADITIONS, 2004

Quantum Shift to the Global Brain
HOW THE NEW SCIENTIFIC REALITY CAN CHANGE US AND OUR WORLD
ROCHESTER: INNER TRADITIONS, 2008

Science and the Reenchantment of the Cosmos
THE RISE OF THE INTEGRAL VISION OF REALITY
ROCHESTER: INNER TRADITIONS, 2006

The Akashic Experience
SCIENCE AND THE COSMIC MEMORY FIELD
ROCHESTER: INNER TRADITIONS, 2009

The Chaos Point
THE WORLD AT THE CROSSROADS
NEWBURYPORT, MA: HAMPTON ROADS PUBLISHING, 2006

LAUD, ANNE & GILSTROP, MAY

Violence in the Family
A SELECTED BIBLIOGRAPHY ON CHILD ABUSE, SEXUAL ABUSE OF
CHILDREN & DOMESTIC VIOLENCE
JUNE 1985
UNIVERSITY OF GEORGIA LIBRARIES
BIBLIOGRAPHICAL SERIES, NO. 32

LEADBEATER, CHARLES WEBSTER

Astral Plane
ITS SCENERY, INHABITANTS AND PHENOMENA
KESSINGER PUBLISHING REPRINT EDITION, 1997

Dreams
WHAT THEY ARE AND HOW THEY ARE CAUSED
LONDON: THEOSOPHICAL PUBLISHING SOCIETY, 1903
KESSINGER PUBLISHING REPRINT EDITION, 1998

The Inner Life
CHICAGO: THE RAJPUT PRESS, 1911
KESSINGER PUBLISHING

LEARY, TIMOTHY

Our Brain is God
BERKELEY, CA: RONIN PUBLISHING, 2001
AUTHOR COPYRIGHT 1988

LEBOYER, FREDERICK

Birth Without Violence
NEW YORK, 1975

Inner Beauty, Inner Light
NEW YORK: NEWMARKET PRESS, 1997

Loving Hands
THE TRADITIONAL ART OF BABY MASSAGE
NEW YORK: NEWMARKET PRESS, 1977

The Art of Breathing
NEW YORK: NEWMARKET PRESS, 1991

LEGGETT, TREVOR P.

A First Zen Reader
RUTLAND: C.E. TUTTLE, 1980
ORIGINALLY PUBLISHED IN 1972

BIBLIOGRAPHY

LEONARD, GEORGE, MURPHY, MICHAEL

The Live We Are Given
A LONG TERM PROGRAM FOR REALIZING THE
POTENTIAL OF BODY, MIND, HEART AND SOUL
NEW YORK: JEREMY P. TARCHER/PUTNAM, 1984

LICHT, HANS

Sexual Life in Ancient Greece
NEW YORK: AMS PRESS, 1995

LIEDLOFF, JEAN

Continuum Concept
IN SEARCH OF HAPPINESS LOST
NEW YORK: PERSEUS BOOKS, 1986
FIRST PUBLISHED IN 1977

LIPTON, BRUCE

The Biology of Belief
UNLEASHING THE POWER OF CONSCIOUSNESS, MATTER AND MIRACLES
SANTA ROSA, CA: MOUNTAIN OF LOVE/ELITE BOOKS, 2005

LOCKE, JOHN

Some Thoughts Concerning Education
LONDON, 1690
REPRINTED IN: THE WORKS OF JOHN LOCKE, 1823
VOL. IX., PP. 6-205

LONG, MAX FREEDOM

The Secret Science at Work
THE HUNA METHOD AS A WAY OF LIFE
MARINA DEL REY: DE VORSS PUBLICATIONS, 1995
ORIGINALLY PUBLISHED IN 1953

Growing Into Light
A PERSONAL GUIDE TO PRACTICING THE HUNA METHOD,
MARINA DEL REY: DE VORSS PUBLICATIONS, 1955

LOWEN, ALEXANDER

Bioenergetics
NEW YORK: COWARD, McGOEGHAM 1975

Depression and the Body
THE BIOLOGICAL BASIS OF FAITH AND REALITY
NEW YORK: PENGUIN, 1992

Fear of Life
NEW YORK: BIOENERGETIC PRESS, 2003

Honoring the Body
THE AUTOBIOGRAPHY OF ALEXANDER LOWEN
NEW YORK: BIOENERGETIC PRESS, 2004

Joy
THE SURRENDER TO THE BODY AND TO LIFE
NEW YORK: PENGUIN, 1995

Love and Orgasm
NEW YORK: MACMILLAN, 1965

Love, Sex and Your Heart
NEW YORK: BIOENERGETICS PRESS, 2004

Narcissism: Denial of the True Self
NEW YORK: MACMILLAN, COLLIER BOOKS, 1983

Pleasure: A Creative Approach to Life
NEW YORK: BIOENERGETICS PRESS, 2004
FIRST PUBLISHED IN 1970

The Language of the Body
PHYSICAL DYNAMICS OF CHARACTER STRUCTURE
NEW YORK: BIOENERGETICS PRESS, 2006

MAHARSHI, RAMANA

The Collected Works of Ramana Maharshi
NEW YORK: SRI RAMANASRAMAM, 2002

The Essential Teachings of Ramana Maharshi
A VISUAL JOURNEY
NEW YORK: INNER DIRECTIONS PUBLISHING, 2002
BY MATTHEW GREENBLAD

MALACHI, TAU

Gnosis of the Cosmic Christ
A GNOSTIC CHRISTIAN KABBALAH
ST. PAUL: LLEWELLYN PUBLICATIONS, 2005

MALINOWSKI, BRONISLAW

Crime und Custom in Savage Society
LONDON: KEGAN, 1926

Sex and Repression in Savage Society
LONDON: KEGAN, 1927

The Sexual Life of Savages in North West Melanesia
NEW YORK: HALYCON HOUSE, 1929

MANN, EDWARD W.

Orgone, Reich & Eros
WILHELM REICH'S THEORY OF LIFE ENERGY
NEW YORK: SIMON & SCHUSTER (TOUCHSTONE), 1973

MARTINSON, FLOYD M.

Sexual Knowledge
VALUES AND BEHAVIOR PATTERNS
ST. PETER: MINN.: GUSTAVUS ADOLPHUS COLLEGE, 1966

Infant and Child Sexuality
ST. PETER: MINN.: GUSTAVUS ADOLPHUS COLLEGE, 1973

The Quality of Adolescent Experiences
ST. PETER: MINN.: GUSTAVUS ADOLPHUS COLLEGE, 1974

The Child and the Family
CALGARY, ALBERTA: THE UNIVERSITY OF CALGARY, 1980

The Sex Education of Young Children
IN: LORNA BROWN (ED.), SEX EDUCATION IN THE EIGHTIES
NEW YORK, LONDON: PLENUM PRESS, 1981, PP. 51 FF.

The Sexual Life of Children
NEW YORK: BERGIN & GARVEY, 1994

Children and Sex, Part II: Childhood Sexuality
IN: BULLOUGH & BULLOUGH, HUMAN SEXUALITY (1994)
PP. 111-116

MASTERS, R.E.L.

Forbidden Sexual Behavior and Morality
NEW YORK, 1962

McCAREY, WILLIAM A.

In Search of Healing
WHOLE-BODY HEALING THROUGH THE MIND-BODY-SPIRIT
CONNECTION
NEW YORK: BERKLEY PUBLISHING, 1996

McLEOD, KEMBREW

Freedom of Expression
RESISTANCE AND REPRESSION IN THE AGE OF INTELLECTUAL PROPERTY
MINNEAPOLIS, MN: UNIVERSITY OF MINNESOTA PRESS, 2007

McNIFF, SHAUN

Art as Medicine
BOSTON: SHAMBHALA, 1992

Art as Therapy
CREATING A THERAPY OF THE IMAGINATION
BOSTON/LONDON: SHAMBHALA, 1992

Trust the Process
AN ARTIST'S GUIDE TO LETTING GO
NEW YORK: SHAMBHALA PUBLICATIONS, 1998

McTAGGART, LYNNE

The Field
THE QUEST FOR THE SECRET FORCE OF THE UNIVERSE
NEW YORK: HARPER & COLLINS, 2002

MEAD, MARGARET

Sex and Temperament in Three Primitive Societies
NEW YORK, 1935

MEADOWS, DONELLA H.

Thinking in Systems
A PRIMER
WHITE RIVER, VT: CHELSEA GREEN PUBLISHING, 2008

MEHTA, ROHIT

J. Krishnamurti and the Nameless Experience
A COMPREHENSIVE DISCUSSION OF J. KRISHNAMURTI'S APPROACH TO
LIFE
DELHI: MOTILAL BANARSIDASS PUBLISHERS, 2002

MERLEAU-PONTY, MAURICE

Phenomenology of Perception
LONDON: ROUTLEDGE, 1995
ORIGINALLY PUBLISHED 1945

METZNER, RALPH (ED.)

Ayahuasca, Human Consciousness and the Spirits of Nature
ED. BY RALPH METZNER, PH.D
NEW YORK: THUNDER'S MOUTH PRESS, 1999

The Psychedelic Experience
A MANUAL BASED ON THE TIBETAN BOOK OF THE DEAD
WITH TIMOTHY LEARY AND RICHARD ALPERT
NEW YORK: CITADEL, 1995

MILLER, ALICE

Four Your Own Good
HIDDEN CRUELTY IN CHILD-REARING AND THE ROOTS OF VIOLENCE
NEW YORK: FARRAR, STRAUS & GIROUX, 1983

Pictures of a Childhood
NEW YORK: FARRAR, STRAUS & GIROUX, 1986

The Drama of the Gifted Child
IN SEARCH FOR THE TRUE SELF
TRANSLATED BY RUTH WARD
NEW YORK: BASIC BOOKS, 1996

Thou Shalt Not Be Aware
SOCIETY'S BETRAYAL OF THE CHILD
NEW YORK: NOONDAY, 1998

The Political Consequences of Child Abuse
IN: THE JOURNAL OF PSYCHOHISTORY 26, 2 (FALL 1998)

MOLL, ALBERT

The Sexual Life of the Child
NEW YORK: MACMILLAN, 1912
FIRST PUBLISHED IN GERMAN AS
DAS SEXUALLEBEN DES KINDES, 1909

MONROE, ROBERT

Ultimate Journey
NEW YORK: BROADWAY BOOKS, 1994

MONSAINGEON, BRUNO

Svjatoslav Richter
NOTEBOOKS AND CONVERSATIONS
PRINCETON: PRINCETON UNIVERSITY PRESS, 2002

Richter The Enigma / L'Insoumis / Der Unbeugsame
NVC ARTS 1998 (DVD)

MONTAGU, ASHLEY

Touching
THE HUMAN SIGNIFICANCE OF THE SKIN
NEW YORK: HARPER & ROW, 1978

BIBLIOGRAPHY

MONTESSORI, MARIA

The Absorbent Mind
REPRINT EDITION
NEW YORK: BUCCANEER BOOKS, 1995
FIRST PUBLISHED IN 1973

MOORE, THOMAS

Care of the Soul
A GUIDE FOR CULTIVATING DEPTH AND SACREDNESS IN EVERYDAY LIFE
NEW YORK: HARPER & COLLINS, 1994

MOSER, CHARLES ALLEN

DSM-IV-TR and the Paraphilias: an argument for removal
WITH PEGGY J. KLEINPLATZ
JOURNAL OF PSYCHOLOGY AND HUMAN SEXUALITY 17 (3/4), 91-109
(2005)

MURDOCK, G.

Social Structure
NEW YORK: MACMILLAN, 1960

MURPHY, JOSEPH

The Power of Your Subconscious Mind
WEST NYACK, N.Y.: PARKER, 1981, N.Y.: BANTAM, 1982
ORIGINALLY PUBLISHED IN 1962

The Miracle of Mind Dynamics
NEW YORK: PRENTICE HALL, 1964

Miracle Power for Infinite Riches
WEST NYACK, N.Y.: PARKER, 1972

The Amazing Laws of Cosmic Mind Power
WEST NYACK, N.Y.: PARKER, 1973

Secrets of the I Ching
WEST NYACK, N.Y.: PARKER, 1970

Think Yourself Rich
USE THE POWER OF YOUR SUBCONSCIOUS MIND TO FIND TRUE WEALTH
REVISED BY IAN D. MCMAHAN, PH.D.
PARAMUS, NJ: REWARD BOOKS, 2001

MURPHY, MICHAEL

The Future of the Body
EXPLORATIONS INTO THE FURTHER EVOLUTION OF HUMAN NATURE
NEW YORK: JEREMY P. TARCHER/PUTNAM, 1992

MYERS, TONY PEARCE

The Soul of Creativity
INSIGHTS INTO THE CREATIVE PROCESS
NOVATO, CA: NEW WORLD LIBRARY, 1999

Myss, Caroline

The Creation of Health
The Emotional, Psychological, and Spiritual Responses that Promote
Health and Healing
New York: Three Rivers Press, 1998

Naparstek, Belleruth

Your Sixth Sense
Unlocking the Power of Your Intuition
London: HarperCollins, 1998

Staying Well With Guided Imagery
New York: Warner Books, 1995

Narby, Jeremy

The Cosmic Serpent
DNA and the Origins of Knowledge
New York: J. P. Tarcher, 1999

Nau, Erika

Self-Awareness Through Huna
Virginia Beach: Donning, 1981

NEILL, ALEXANDER SUTHERLAND

Neill! Neill! Orange-Peel!
NEW YORK: HART PUBLISHING CO., 1972

Summerhill
A RADICAL APPROACH TO CHILD REARING
NEW YORK: HART PUBLISHING, REPRINT 1984
ORIGINALLY PUBLISHED 1960

Summerhill School
A NEW VIEW OF CHILDHOOD
NEW YORK: ST. MARTIN'S PRESS
REPRINT 1995

NEUMANN, ERICH

The Great Mother
PRINCETON: PRINCETON UNIVERSITY PRESS, 1955
(BOLLINGEN SERIES)

NEWTON, MICHAEL

Life Between Lives
HYPNOTHERAPY FOR SPIRITUAL REGRESSION
WOODBURY, MINN.: LLEWELLYN PUBLICATIONS, 2006

NICHOLS, SALLIE

Jung and Tarot: An Archetypal Journey
NEW YORK: RED WHEEL/WEISER, 1986

NIN, ANAÏS

The Diary of Anaïs Nin (7 Volumes)
NEW YORK, 1966

Volume 1 (1931-1934)
NEW YORK: HARVEST BOOKS, 1969

Volume 2 (1934-1939)
NEW YORK: HARVEST BOOKS, 1970

ODENT, MICHEL

Birth Reborn
WHAT CHILDBIRTH SHOULD BE
LONDON: SOUVENIR PRESS, 1994

The Scientification of Love
LONDON: FREE ASSOCIATION BOOKS, 1999

Primal Health
UNDERSTANDING THE CRITICAL PERIOD BETWEEN CONCEPTION
AND THE FIRST BIRTHDAY
LONDON: CLAIRVIEW BOOKS, 2002
FIRST PUBLISHED IN 1986 WITH CENTURY HUTCHINSON IN LONDON

The Functions of the Orgasms
THE HIGHWAY TO TRANSCENDENCE
LONDON: PINTER & MARTIN, 2009

OLLENDORF-REICH, ILSE

Wilhelm Reich, A Personal Biography
NEW YORK, ST. MARTINS PRESS, 1969

Wilhelm Reich
VORWORT VON A.S. NEILL
MÜNCHEN, KINDLER, 1975

PEARCE MYERS, TONY (EDITOR)

The Soul of Creativity
INSIGHTS INTO THE CREATIVE PROCESS
NOVATO: NEW WORLD LIBRARY, 1999

PERT, CANDACE B.

Molecules of Emotion
THE SCIENCE BEHIND MIND-BODY MEDICINE
NEW YORK: SCRIBNER, 2003

PETRASH, JACK

Understanding Waldorf Education
TEACHING FROM THE INSIDE OUT
LONDON: FLORIS BOOKS, 2003

PLUMMER, KENNETH

Pedophilia
CONSTRUCTING A SOCIOLOGICAL BASELINE
IN: IN: COOK, M. AND HOWELLS, K. (EDS.):
ADULT SEXUAL INTEREST IN CHILDREN
ACADEMIC PRESS, LONDON, 1980, PP. 220 FF.

PORTEOUS, HEDY S.

Sex and Identity
YOUR CHILD'S SEXUALITY
INDIANAPOLIS: BOBBS-MERRILL, 1972

PRESCOTT, JAMES W.

Affectional Bonding for the Prevention of Violent Behaviors
NEUROBIOLOGICAL, PSYCHOLOGICAL AND RELIGIOUS/SPIRITUAL
DETERMINANTS, IN: HERTZBERG, L.J., OSTRUM, G.F. AND FIELD, J.R.,
(EDS.)

Violent Behavior
VOL. 1, ASSESSMENT & INTERVENTION, CHAPTER SIX
NEW YORK: PMA PUBLISHING, 1990

Alienation of Affection
PSYCHOLOGY TODAY, DECEMBER 1979

Body Pleasure and the Origins of Violence
BULLETIN OF THE ATOMIC SCIENTISTS, 10-20 (1975)

*Deprivation of Physical Affection as a Primary Process in the
Development of Physical Violence A Comparative and
Cross-Cultural Perspective, in: David G. Gil, ed., Child Abuse and
Violence*
NEW YORK: AMS PRESS, 1979

*Early somatosensory deprivation as an ontogenetic process in
the abnormal development of the brain and behavior,*
IN: MEDICAL PRIMATOLOGY, ED. BY I.E. GOLDSMITH AND J.
MOOR-JANKOWSKI,
NEW YORK: S. KARGER, 1971

Genital Mutilation of Children: Failure of Humanity and Humanism
UNPRINTED ESSAY (2005)
HTTP://WWW.VIOLENCE.DE/PRESCOTT/LETTERS/
CIRC_CONGRESS_MONTAGUE_9.30.05.HTML

Genital Pain vs. Genital Pleasure
WHY THE ONE AND NOT THE OTHER
THE TRUTH SEEKER, JULY/AUGUST 1989, PP. 14-21
HTTP://WWW.VIOLENCE.DE/PRESCOTT/TRUTHSEEKER/GENPL.HTML

How Culture Shapes the Developing Brain and the Future of Humanity
A BRIEF SUMMARY OF THE RESEARCH WHICH LINKS BRAIN ABNORMALITIES AND VIOLENCE TO AN ABSENCE OF NURTURING AND BONDING VERY EARLY IN CHILDHOOD, IN: TOUCH THE FUTURE: OPTIMUM LEARNING RELATIONSHIPS

for Children & Adults
SPRING 2002 (ED. BY MICHAEL MENDIZZA)
NEVADA CITY, CA, 2002

Invited Commentary: Central nervous system functioning in altered sensory environments
IN: M.H. APPLEY AND R. TRUMBULL (EDS.), PSYCHOLOGICAL STRESS, NEW YORK: APPLETON-CENTURY CROFTS, 1967

Our Two Cultural Brains: Neurointegrative and Neurodissociative
HTTP://WWW.VIOLENCE.DE/PRESCOTT/LETTERS/OUR_TWO_CULTURAL_BRAINS.PDF

Phylogenetic and ontogenetic aspects of human affectional development,
IN: PROGRESS IN SEXOLOGY, PROCEEDINGS OF THE 1976 INTERNATIONAL, CONGRESS OF SEXOLOGY, ED. BY R. GEMME & C.C. WHEELER, NEW YORK: PLENUM PRESS, 1977

Prevention or Therapy and the Politics of Trust Inspiring a New Human Agenda
IN: PSYCHOTHERAPY AND POLITICS INTERNATIONAL
VOLUME 3(3), PP. 194-211
LONDON: JOHN WILEY, 2005

Sex and the Brain
MIDCONTINENT & EASTERN REGIONS, JUNE 13-16, 2002
BIG RAPIDS, MI: SOCIETY FOR CROSS-CULTURAL RESEARCH,
32ND ANNUAL MEETING, 2005
HTTP://WWW.VIOLENCE.DE/ARCHIVE.SHTML

Sixteen Principles for Personal, Family and Global Peace
THE TRUTH SEEKER, MARCH/APRIL 1989
HTTP://WWW.VIOLENCE.DE/PRESCOTT/LETTERS/SIXTEEN_PRINCIPLES.PDF

Somatosensory affectional deprivation (SAD) theory of drug and alcohol use
IN: THEORIES ON DRUG ABUSE: SELECTED CONTEMPORARY
PERSPECTIVES, ED. BY DAN J. LETTIERI, MOLLIE SAYERS AND HELEN
WALLENSTIEN PEARSON, NIDA RESEARCH MONOGRAPH 30, MARCH
1980, ROCKVILLE, MD: NATIONAL INSTITUTE ON DRUG ABUSE,
DEPARTMENT OF HEALTH AND HUMAN SERVICES, 1980

The Origins of Human Love and Violence
PRE- AND PERINATAL PSYCHOLOGY JOURNAL, VOLUME 10, NUMBER 3:
SPRING 1996, PP. 143-188THE ORIGINS OF LOVE AND VIOLENCE

Sensory Deprivation and the Developing Brain
RESEARCH AND PREVENTION (DVD)
HTTP://TTFUTURE.ORG/STORE/ORIGINS_ORDERS
HTTP://VIOLENCE.DE
HTTP://TTFUTURE.ORG/VIOLENCE
HTTP://MONTAGUNOCIRCPETITION.ORG

PRITCHARD, COLIN

The Child Abusers
NEW YORK: OPEN UNIVERSITY PRESS, 2004

RAKNES, OLA

Wilhelm Reich and Orgonomy
OSLO: UNIVERSITETSFORLAGET, 1970

RANDALL, NEVILLE

Life After Death
LONDON: ROBERT HALE, 1999

RANK, OTTO

Art and Artist
WITH CHARLES FRANCIS ATKINSON AND ANAÏS NIN
NEW YORK: W.W. NORTON, 1989
ORIGINALLY PUBLISHED IN 1932

The Significance of Psychoanalysis for the Mental Sciences
NEW YORK: BIBLIOBAZAAR, 2009
FIRST PUBLISHED IN 1913

REDFIELD, JAMES

The Tenth Insight
HOLDING THE VISION
NEW YORK: WARNER BOOKS, 1996

BIBLIOGRAPHY

The Celestine Prophecy
NEW YORK: WARNER BOOKS, 1995

REICH, WILHELM

A Review of the Theories, dating from The 17th Century, on the Origin of Organic Life
BY ARTHUR HAHN, LITERATURE ASSISTANT AT THE INSTITUT FÜR SEXUALÖKONOMISCHE LEBENSFORSCHUNG, BIOLOGISCHES LABORATORIUM, OSLO, 1938, ©1979 MARY BOYD HIGGINS AS DIRECTOR OF THE WILHELM REICH INFANT TRUST, XEROX COPY FROM THE WILHELM REICH MUSEUM

Children of the Future
ON THE PREVENTION OF SEXUAL PATHOLOGY
NEW YORK: FARRAR, STRAUS & GIROUX, 1984
FIRST PUBLISHED IN 1950

CORE (Cosmic Orgone Engineering)
PART I, SPACE SHIPS, DOR AND DROUGHT
©1984, ORGONE INSTITUTE PRESS
XEROX COPY FROM THE WILHELM REICH MUSEUM
KÖLN: KIEPENHEUER & WITSCH, 1987

Early Writings 1
NEW YORK: FARRAR, STRAUS & GIROUX, 1975

Ether, God & Devil & Cosmic Superimposition
NEW YORK: FARRAR, STRAUS & GIROUX, 1972
ORIGINALLY PUBLISHED IN 1949

Genitality in the Theory and Therapy of Neurosis
©1980 BY MARY BOYD HIGGINS AS DIRECTOR OF THE WILHELM REICH INFANT TRUST

People in Trouble
©1974 BY MARY BOYD HIGGINS AS DIRECTOR OF THE WILHELM REICH
INFANT TRUST

Record of a Friendship
THE CORRESPONDENCE OF WILHELM REICH AND A. S. NEILL
NEW YORK, FARRAR, STRAUS & GIROUX, 1981

Selected Writings
AN INTRODUCTION TO ORGONOMY
NEW YORK: FARRAR, STRAUS & GIROUX, 1973

The Bioelectrical Investigation of Sexuality and Anxiety
NEW YORK: FARRAR, STRAUS & GIROUX, 1983
ORIGINALLY PUBLISHED IN 1935

The Bion Experiments
REPRINTED IN SELECTED WRITINGS
NEW YORK: FARRAR, STRAUS & GIROUX, 1973

The Cancer Biopathy (The Orgone, Vol. 2)
NEW YORK: FARRAR, STRAUS & GIROUX, 1973

The Function of the Orgasm (The Orgone, Vol. 1)
ORGONE INSTITUTE PRESS, NEW YORK, 1942

The Invasion of Compulsory Sex Morality
NEW YORK: FARRAR, STRAUS & GIROUX, 1971
ORIGINALLY PUBLISHED IN 1932

The Leukemia Problem: Approach
©1951, ORGONE INSTITUTE PRESS
COPYRIGHT RENEWED 1979
XEROX COPY FROM THE WILHELM REICH MUSEUM

BIBLIOGRAPHY

The Mass Psychology of Fascism
NEW YORK: FARRAR, STRAUS & GIROUX, 1970
ORIGINALLY PUBLISHED IN 1933

The Orgone Energy Accumulator
ITS SCIENTIFIC AND MEDICAL USE
©1951, 1979, ORGONE INSTITUTE PRESS
XEROX COPY FROM THE WILHELM REICH MUSEUM

The Schizophrenic Split
©1945, 1949, 1972 BY MARY BOYD HIGGINS AS DIRECTOR OF THE
WILHELM REICH INFANT TRUST
XEROX COPY FROM THE WILHELM REICH MUSEUM

The Sexual Revolution
©1945, 1962 BY MARY BOYD HIGGINS AS DIRECTOR OF THE
WILHELM REICH INFANT TRUST

RISO, DON RICHARD & HUDSON, RUSS

The Wisdom of the Enneagram
THE COMPLETE GUIDE TO PSYCHOLOGICAL AND SPIRITUAL GROWTH
FOR THE NINE PERSONALITY TYPES
NEW YORK: BANTAM BOOKS, 1999

ROBBINS, ANTHONY

Awaken The Giant Within
NEW YORK: SIMON & SCHUSTER, 1991

Unlimited Power
THE NEW SCIENCE OF PERSONAL ACHIEVEMENT
NEW YORK: FREE PRESS, 1997

ROBERTS, JANE

The Nature of Personal Reality
NEW YORK: AMBER-ALLEN PUBLISHING, 1994
FIRST PUBLISHED IN 1974

The Nature of the Psyche
ITS HUMAN EXPRESSION
NEW YORK, AMBER-ALLEN PUBLISHING, 1996
FIRST PUBLISHED IN 1979

ROSEN, SYDNEY (ED.)

My Voice Will Go With You
THE TEACHING TALES OF MILTON H. ERICKSON
NEW YORK: NORTON & CO., 1991

ROTHSCHILD & WOLF

Children of the Counterculture
NEW YORK: GARDEN CITY, 1976

SANDFORT, THEO

The Sexual Aspect of Pedophile Relations
THE EXPERIENCE OF TWENTY-FIVE BOYS
AMSTERDAM: PAN/SPARTACUS, 1982

SCHLIPP, PAUL A. (ED.)

Albert Einstein
PHILOSOPHER-SCIENTIST
NEW YORK: OPEN COURT PUBLISHING, 1988

SCHWARTZ, ANDREW E.

Guided Imagery for Groups
FIFTY VISUALIZATIONS THAT PROMOTE RELAXATION, PROBLEM-SOLVING,
CREATIVITY, AND WELL-BEING
WHOLE PERSON ASSOCIATES, 1995

SHARAF, MYRON

Fury on Earth
A BIOGRAPHY OF WILHELM REICH
LONDON: ANDRÉ DEUTSCH, 1983

SHELDRAKE, RUPERT

A New Science of Life
THE HYPOTHESIS OF MORPHIC RESONANCE
ROCHESTER: PARK STREET PRESS, 1995

SHER, BARBARA & GOTTLIEB, ANNIE

Wishcraft
HOW TO GET WHAT YOU REALLY WANT
2ND EDITION, NEW YORK: BALLANTINE BOOKS, 2003

SHONE, RONALD

Creative Visualization
USING IMAGERY AND IMAGINATION FOR SELF-TRANSFORMATION
NEW YORK: DESTINY BOOKS, 1998

SIMONTON, O. CARL ET AL.

Getting Well Again
LOS ANGELES: TARCHER, 1978

SINGER, JUNE

Androgyny
NEW YORK: DOUBLEDAY DELL, 1976

SMITH, C. MICHAEL

Jung and Shamanism in Dialogue
LONDON: TRAFFORD PUBLISHING, 2007

SPOCK, BENJAMIN

Dr. Spock's Baby and Child Care
8TH EDITION
NEW YORK: POCKET BOOKS, 2004

STEIN, ROBERT M.

Redeeming the Inner Child in Marriage and Therapy
IN: RECLAIMING THE INNER CHILD
ED. BY JEREMIAH ABRAMS
NEW YORK: TARCHER/PUTNAM, 1990, 261 FF.

STEINER, RUDOLF

Theosophy
AN INTRODUCTION TO THE SPIRITUAL PROCESSES IN HUMAN LIFE
AND IN THE COSMOS
NEW YORK: ANTHROPOSOPHIC PRESS, 1994

STEKEL, WILHELM

Auto-Eroticism
A PSYCHIATRIC STUDY OF ONANISM AND NEUROSIS
REPUBLISHED, LONDON: PAUL KEGAN, 2004

Patterns of Psychosexual Infantilism
NEW YORK, 1959 (REPRINT EDITION)

Sadism and Masochism
NEW YORK: W.W. NORTON & CO., 1953

Sex and Dreams
THE LANGUAGE OF DREAMS
REPUBLISHED
NEW YORK: UNIVERSITY PRESS OF THE PACIFIC, 2003

Stiene, Bronwen & Frans

The Reiki Sourcebook
New York: O Books, 2003

The Japanese Art of Reiki
A Practical Guide to Self-Healing
New York: O Books, 2005

Stone, Hal & Stone, Sidra

Embracing Our Selves
The Voice Dialogue Manual
San Rafael, CA: New World Library, 1989

Strassman, Rick

DMT: The Spirit Molecule
A doctor's revolutionary research into the biology of
near-death and mystical experiences
Rochester: Park Street Press, 2001

Symonds, John Addington

A Problem in Greek Ethics
New York: M.S.G. House, 1971

Szasz, Thomas

The Myth of Mental Illness
New York: Harper & Row, 1984

TALBOT, MICHAEL

The Holographic Universe
NEW YORK: HARPERCOLLINS, 1992

TARNAS, RICHARD

Cosmos and Psyche
INTIMATIONS OF A NEW WORLD VIEW
NEW YORK: PLUME, 2007

The Passion of the Western Mind
UNDERSTANDING THE IDEAS THAT HAVE SHAPED OUR WORLD VIEW
NEW YORK: BALLANTINE BOOKS, 1993

TART, CHARLES T.

Altered States of Consciousness
A BOOK OF READINGS
HOBOKEN, N.J.: WILEY & SONS, 1969

TEXTOR, R. B.

A Cross-Cultural Summary
NEW HAVEN, HUMAN RELATIONS AREA FILES (HRAF)
PRESS, 1967

THE ADVENT OF GREAT AWAKENING

A Course in Miracles
TEXT WORKBOOK AND MANUAL FOR TEACHERS

New York: New Christian Church of Full Endeavor, 2007

Tiller, William A.

Conscious Acts of Creation
The Emergence of a New Physics
Associated Producers, 2004 (DVD)

Psychoenergetic Science
New York: Pavior, 2007

Toffler, Alvin

Powershift
Knowledge, Wealth, and Violence at the Edge of the 21st Century
New York: Bantam, 1991

Revolutionary Wealth
How it will be created and how it will change our lives
New York: Broadway Business, 2007

The Third Wave
New York: Bantam, 1984

Tolle, Eckhart

The Power of Now
A Guide to Spiritual Enlightenment
Novato, CA: New World Library, 2004

A New Earth: Awakening to Your Life's Purpose
NEW YORK: MICHAEL JOSEPH (PENGUIN), 2005

UNLAWFUL SEX

Offences, Victims and Offenders in the Criminal Justice System of England and Wales
THE REPORT OF THE HOWARD LEAGUE WORKING PARTY
LONDON: WATERLOO PUBLISHERS LTD., 1985

VILLOLDO, ALBERTO

Healing States
A JOURNEY INTO THE WORLD OF SPIRITUAL HEALING AND SHAMANISM
WITH STANLEY KRIPPNER
NEW YORK: SIMON & SCHUSTER (FIRESIDE), 1987

Dance of the Four Winds: Secrets of the Inca Medicine Wheel
WITH ERIC JENDRESEN
ROCHESTER: DESTINY BOOKS, 1995

Shaman, Healer, Sage
HOW TO HEAL YOURSELF AND OTHERS WITH THE ENERGY MEDICINE
OF THE AMERICAS
NEW YORK: HARMONY, 2000

Healing the Luminous Body
THE WAY OF THE SHAMAN WITH DR. ALBERTO VILLOLDO
DVD, SACRED MYSTERIES PRODUCTIONS, 2004

Mending The Past And Healing The Future with Soul Retrieval
NEW YORK: HAY HOUSE, 2005

WARD, ELIZABETH

Father-Daughter Rape
NEW YORK: GROVE PRESS, 1985

WHARTON

Wharton's Criminal Law
14TH ED. BY CHARLES E. TORCIA
VOL. II, §§99-282
ROCHESTER, NEW YORK: THE LAWYERS COOPERATIVE PUBLISHING CO.,
1979

WHITFIELD, CHARLES L.

Healing the Child Within
DEERFIELD BEACH, FL: HEALTH COMMUNICATIONS, 1987

WHITING, BEATRICE B.

Children of Six Cultures
A PSYCHO-CULTURAL ANALYSIS
CAMBRIDGE: HARVARD UNIVERSITY PRESS, 1975

WILBER, KEN

Sex, Ecology, Spirituality
THE SPIRIT OF EVOLUTION
BOSTON: SHAMBHALA, 2000

Quantum Questions
MYSTICAL WRITINGS OF THE WORLD'S GREATEST PHYSICISTS
BOSTON: SHAMBHALA, 2001

WILLIAMS, STREPHON KAPLAN

Dreams and Spiritual Growth
WITH PATRICIA H. BERNE AND LOUIS M. SAVARY
NEW YORK: PAULIST PRESS, 1984

Dream Cards
UNDERSTAND YOUR DREAMS AND ENRICH YOUR LIFE
NEW YORK: SIMON & SCHUSTER (FIRESIDE), 1991

WOLF, FRED ALAN

Taking the Quantum Leap
THE NEW PHYSICS FOR NONSCIENTISTS
NEW YORK: HARPER & ROW, 1989

Parallel Universes
NEW YORK: SIMON & SCHUSTER, 1990

The Dreaming Universe
A MIND-EXPANDING JOURNEY INTO THE REALM WHERE PSYCHE AND PHYSICS MEET
NEW YORK: TOUCHSTONE, 1995

The Eagle's Quest
A PHYSICIST FINDS THE SCIENTIFIC TRUTH AT THE HEART OF THE SHAMANIC WORLD
NEW YORK: TOUCHSTONE, 1997

YATES, ALAYNE

Sex Without Shame: Encouraging the Child's Healthy Sexual Development
NEW YORK, 1978
REPUBLISHED INTERNET EDITION

ZUKAV, GARY

The Dancing Wu Li Masters
AN OVERVIEW OF THE NEW PHYSICS
NEW YORK: HARPERONE, 2001

www.ingramcontent.com/pod-product-compliance
Lightning Source LLC
Chambersburg PA
CBHW051045250726
48656CB00001B/151